Teach Now!

The companion website for this series can be found at
www.routledge.com/cw/teachnow. All of the useful web
links highlighted in the book can be found here, along with
additional resources and activities.

*Being taught by a great teacher is one of the great privileges of
life.* Teach Now! *is an exciting new series that opens up the secrets
of great teachers and, step by step, helps trainees to build the skills
and confidence they need to become first-rate classroom practitioners.*

Written by a highly skilled practitioner, this practical, classroom-focused guide contains all the support you need to become a great English teacher. Combining a grounded, modern rationale for learning and teaching with highly practical training approaches, the book guides you through all the different aspects of English teaching, offering clear, straightforward advice on classroom practice, lesson planning and working in schools.

Celebrating the values of English teaching, Alex Quigley sets out a 'steps to success' model that will help you to go from novice to expert teacher. The English curriculum, planning, assessment, behaviour management, literacy and differentiation are all discussed in detail alongside carefully chosen examples to demonstrate good practice. There are also chapters on dealing with pressure, excelling in observations, finding the right job and succeeding at interview. Throughout the book, there is a great selection of ready-to-use activities and techniques, including effective reading and writing strategies, pedagogies for teaching poetry and Shakespeare, and how to harness the power of debate, dialogue and drama, all of which will help you overcome any challenges and put you on the fast track to success in the classroom.

Covering everything you need to know, this book is your essential guide as you start your exciting and rewarding career as an outstanding English teacher.

Alex Quigley is the English Subject Leader and Assistant Head Teacher at Huntington School, York, UK. He has taught English for a decade and he blogs regularly about teaching and learning at www.huntingenglish.com

Teach Now!

Series editor: Geoff Barton

Being taught by a great teacher is one of the great privileges of life. *Teach Now!* is an exciting new series that opens up the secrets of great teachers and, step-by-step, helps trainees to build the skills and confidence they need to become first-rate classroom practitioners. The series comprises a core text that explores what every teacher needs to know about essential issues such as learning, pedagogy, assessment and behaviour management, and subject specific books that guide the reader through the key components and challenges in teaching individual subjects. Written by expert practitioners, the books in this series combine an underpinning philosophy of teaching and learning alongside engaging activities, strategies and techniques to ensure success in the classroom.

Titles in the series:

Teach Now! The Essentials of Teaching
Geoff Barton

Teach Now! History
Becoming a Great History Teacher
Mike Gershon

Teach Now! English
Becoming a Great English Teacher
Alex Quigley

Teach Now! Science
The Joy of Teaching Science
Tom Sherrington

Teach Now! Modern Foreign Languages
Becoming a Great Teacher of Modern Foreign Languages
Sally Allan

Teach Now! Mathematics
Becoming a Great Mathematics Teacher
Julia Upton

Teach Now!
English

Becoming a Great
English Teacher

Alex Quigley

Routledge
Taylor & Francis Group

LONDON AND NEW YORK

First published 2014
by Routledge
2 Park Square, Milton Park, Abingdon, Oxon OX14 4RN

and by Routledge
711 Third Avenue, New York, NY 10017

Routledge is an imprint of the Taylor & Francis Group, an informa business

© 2014 A. Quigley

British Library Cataloguing in Publication Data
A catalogue record for this book is available from the British Library

Library of Congress Cataloging in Publication Data
Quigley, Alex.
   Teach now! English: becoming a great English teacher/Alex Quigley.
   pages cm – (Teach now!)
   1. English language – Study and teaching. 2. English teachers
   –Training of. 3. Language arts. I. Title.
   LB1576.Q54 2014
   428.0071 – dc23
   2013049586

ISBN: 978-0-415-71100-5 (hbk)
ISBN: 978-0-415-71101-2 (pbk)
ISBN: 978-1-315-76900-4 (ebk)

Typeset in Celeste and Optima
by Florence Production Ltd, Stoodleigh, Devon UK

Contents

Contents

Series editor's foreword

What is this series about and who is it for?

Many of us unashamedly like being teachers.

We shrug off the jibes about being in it for the holidays. We ignore the stereotypes in soap operas, sitcoms, bad films and serious news programmes. We don't feel any need to apologise for what we do, despite a constant and corrosive sense of being undervalued.

We always knew that being criticised was part of the deal.

We aren't defensive. We aren't apologetic. We simply like teaching.

And whether we still spend the majority of our working week in the classroom or, as senior leaders, we regard the classroom as a sanctuary from the swirling madness beyond the school gates, we think teaching matters.

We think it matters a lot.

And we think that students need more good teachers.

That's where 'Teach Now!' started as a concept. Could we – as a group of teachers and teaching leaders, scattered across England – put together the kind of books we wish we had had when we were embarking on our own journeys into the secret garden of education.

Of course, there were lots of books around then. Nowadays there are even more – books, plus ebooks, blogs and tweets. You can hardly move on the Internet without tripping over another reflection on a lesson that went well or badly, another teacher extolling a particular approach or dismissing another craze or moaning about the management.

So we know you don't necessarily think you need us. There's plenty of people out there ready to shovel advice and guidance towards a fledgling teacher.

But we wanted to do something different. We wanted to provide two essential texts that would distil our collective knowledge as teachers and package it in a form which was easy to read, authoritative, re-readable, reassuring and deeply rooted in the day-to-day realities of education as it is – not as a consultant or adviser might depict it.

We are writing, in other words, in the early hours of days when each of us will be teaching classes, taking assemblies, watching lessons, looking at schemes of work and dealing with naughty students – and possibly naughty teachers.

We believe this gives our series a distinctive sense of being grounded in the realities of real schools, the kind of places we each work in every day.

We want to provide a warts-and-all account of how to be a great teacher, but we also each believe that education is an essentially optimistic career.

However grim the news out there, in our classrooms we can weave a kind of magic, given the right conditions and the right behaviour. We can reassure ourselves and the students in front of us that, together, we can make the world better.

And if that seems far-fetched, then you haven't seen enough great teachers.

As Roy Blatchford – himself an exceptional teacher and now the Director of the National Education Trust – says in his list of what great teachers do:

> The best teachers are children at heart
> Sitting in the best lessons, you just don't want to leave.
> (Roy Blatchford, *The 2012 Teachers' Standards in the Classroom*, Sage, 2013)

We want young people to experience more lessons like that – classrooms where the sense of time is different, where it expands and shrinks as the world beyond the classroom recedes and where interest and passion and fascination take over; places where whatever your background your brain will fire with new experiences, thoughts and ideas; where whatever your experience so far of the adult world, here, in this classroom, is an adult who cares a lot about something, can communicate it vividly and, in the way she or he talks and behaves, demonstrates a care and interest in you that is remarkable.

We need more classrooms like that and more teachers to take their place within them.

So that's what we have set out to do: to create a series of books that will – if you share our sense of moral purpose – help you to become a great teacher.

You'll have noticed that we expect you to buy two books. We said we were optimistic. That's because we think that being a great teacher has two important dimensions to it. First, you need to know your subject – to really know it.

We know from very good sources that the most effective teachers are experts in what they teach. That doesn't mean they know everything about it. In fact, they often fret about how little they feel they truly know. But they are hungry and passionate and eager – and all those other characteristics that define the teachers who inspire us.

So we know that subject knowledge is really important – and not just for teaching older students. It is as important when teaching Year 7s, knowing what you need to teach and what you can, for now, ignore.

We also believe that subject knowledge is much more than a superficial whisk through key dates or key concepts. It's about having a depth of knowledge that allows us to join up ideas, to explore complexity and nuance, to make decisions about what the key building-blocks of learning a subject might be.

Great teachers sense this and, over a number of years, they build their experience and hone their skills. That's why we have developed subject specialist books for English, mathematics, history, modern foreign languages and science. These are the books that will help you to take what you learnt on your degree course and to think through how to make that knowledge and those skills powerfully effective in the classroom.

They will take you from principles to practice, from philosophy deep into pedagogy. They will help to show you that any terror you may have about becoming a teacher of a subject is inevitable, and that knowing your stuff, careful planning, informed strategies – that all of these will help you to teach now.

Then there's *Teach Now! The Essentials of Teaching*, which is the core text because we also believe that even if you are the best informed scientist, linguist or mathematician in the universe, that this in itself won't make you a great teacher.

That's because great teachers do things that support and supplement their subject knowledge. This is the stuff that the late, great educator Michael Marland called the 'craft of the classroom'. It's what the best teachers know and do instinctively but, to those of us looking on from the outside, or in the earliest stages of a teaching career, can seem mysterious, unattainable, a kind of magic.

It's also the kind of stuff that conventional training may not sufficiently cover.

We're talking about how to open the classroom door, knowing where to stand, knowing what to say to the student who is cheeky, knowing how to survive when you feel, in the darkest of glooms, intimidated by preparation and by marking, that you have made a terrible career choice.

These two texts combined – the subject specialist book and the core book – are designed to help you wherever you are training – in a school or academy or on a PGCE course. Whether you are receiving expert guidance, or it's proving to be more mixed, we hope our ideas, approaches and advice will reassure you, and help you to gain in confidence.

We hope we are providing books that you will want to read and re-read as you train, as you take up your first post and as you finally shrug off the feelings of early insecurity and start to stretch your wings as a fully fledged teacher.

So that's the idea behind the books.

And throughout the writing of them we have been very conscious that – just like us – you have too little time. We have therefore aimed to write in a style that is easy-to-read, reassuring, occasionally provocative and opinionated. We don't want to be bland: teaching is too important for any of us to wilt under a weight of colourless eduspeak.

That's why we have written in short paragraphs, short chapters, added occasional points for reflection and discussion, comments from trainee and veteran teachers, and aimed throughout to create practical, working guides to help you teach now.

So thanks for choosing to read what we have provided. We would love to hear how your early journey into teaching goes and hope that our series helps you on your way into and through a rewarding and enjoyable career.

Geoff Barton
with Sally Allan, Mike Gershon, Alex Quigley, Tom Sherrington and Julia Upton
The *Teach Now!* team of authors

Acknowledgements

Thank you beyond words to Katy, Freya and Noah, for giving me everything I ever wanted or needed. I could not have written this book without you, in so many ways! Thanks to my parents for making me believe I could do things like write this book.

Thanks to the people at Huntington School for giving me the knowledge and experience I needed to write this book, and huge thanks to the many great contributors who kindly added their gems of wisdom that enrich this book.

Thank you to Tom Sherrington for helping me along with our project as fellow new writers (I recommend his book to any scientist teacher friends!). Final thanks go to the brilliant Geoff Barton. You could not find a better guide through the travails of writing a first book. This book is immeasurably better for his sage guidance and editing skill.

Alex Quigley
York, January 2014

Useful acronyms and initialisms – 'an alphabet soup'

ADD	Attention deficit disorder
AF	Assessment foci
AfL	Assessment for learning
APP	Assessing pupils' progress
BESD	Behavioural, emotional and social difficulties
CATs	Cognitive ability tests
CPD	Continued professional development
EAL	English as an additional language
ELS	Early literacy support
FSM	Free school meals
G&T	Gifted and talented
GCSE	General Certificate of Secondary Education (iGCSE: the Cambridge version)
IB	International Baccalaureate
IEP	Individual education plan
LAC	Literacy across the curriculum
LO	Learning objective
NATE	National Association for the Teaching of English
PBL	Project-based learning
PMLD	Profound and multiple learning difficulties
S&L	Speaking and listening
SATs	Standard attainment test
SEN	Special educational needs

Useful acronyms and initialisms

SLD	Severe learning difficulties
SOL	Scheme of learning
SPaG	Spelling, punctuation and grammar
TA	Teaching assistant (HLTA: Higher-level teaching assistant)
TEFL	Teaching English as a foreign language
VI	Visually impaired

1 English curriculum essentials

You may well begin reading this chapter with a fistful of questions. What exactly constitutes the English curriculum? Does it resemble my own school experience? Put simply, with no doubt some trepidation, *what do I need to know?*

This chapter will hopefully provide many of the answers you need, while provoking some new, even more useful questions.

The English curriculum is at once reassuringly familiar and at the same time incredibly wide ranging in its scope. In this chapter, the aim is to identify and distil the essential knowledge and skills required to teach English, so that you can enter the classroom with confidence. We will cover the broadly known basics of reading, writing and why teaching Shakespeare to a bunch of bored teenagers isn't as insurmountable as it may first appear.

If you were to read the newspapers and listen to the siren calls of the media, you would be right to have your sense of confidence and belief in teaching English dented. Stories in the press easily demonise the decline of the English language. Grammar has apparently been irreparably broken by the onslaught of technology. Reading for pleasure is withering on the vine, and the very standard of children's writing is in inexorable decline. Who would enter such a profession at such a time?

Well, me. And you. There are also many thousands of fellow English teachers who are still happy to haul themselves up the barricades. School leaders, parents, charities and politicians are responding to the challenges of falling literacy. For myself, despite the swirling media tales of gloom, and after over a decade of teaching English, I have never felt so optimistic about the job.

You too should be reading this book with excitement and brimming with confidence as you embark upon your teaching career. Too much of the cynicism in the media is founded upon polarising debates over issues such as the supposed decline of grammar, perpetual changes in the English curriculum and the shackling of learning at the hands of stifling examinations.

We must steel ourselves in the midst of such rhetoric and simply get on in our classrooms with inspiring a love of reading and a love of English in its rich diversity.

My optimism derives from my deep-rooted sense of purpose about the teaching of English. The same drive and passion that led me into teaching English in the first place, over a decade ago. The debates that surround English take on a secondary importance in the face of the knowledge that learning English provides essential tools for literacy, and it can give life-long emotional nourishment to the students in our care.

It is worth considering what purpose brought you to the brink of teaching English. Ask yourself: How will you cultivate and retain such optimism in the face of trials and a torrent of late-night marking? What did your experience of learning English teach you? What kindled your passion for English, and how can you pass that on?

The effective teaching of reading

The importance of reading is one of those universal truths upon which everyone can agree. In considering what passion brought to you to teaching English in the first place, many of you will find the answer was rooted in a deep love of reading. Something that changed you and opened up a world of imaginative opportunities that you have the urge to share.

Reading begins long before students enter the English classroom, of course. It is most typically rooted in the earliest of years. Reading with parents or family members creates long-lasting memories and can ensure a lifelong love of reading. From a very early age, reading is imperative. Robert K. Merton coined the sociological concept of 'The Matthew Effect', from the Biblical reference that explains that 'the rich get rich and the poor get poorer'. This applies to language use and reading, where the 'word rich' get richer, whereas the 'word poor' get poorer. From birth, some children read less with parents, fall behind at school and, cumulatively over time, read far less than their more proficient peers.

The gap in vocabulary between the *word rich* and the *word poor* is daunting. Studies by the Department of Education have indicated the gap stretches to many thousands of words between different students – even as early as seven years of age. If this wealth and breadth of words become effective predictors of broader success in education, then we clearly have a crucial task at hand.

It is our role to attempt to close that vocabulary gap. This task takes many forms. We need to help students with weak literacy to decode words more effectively. We need to know what strategies best suit this task – from 'reading recovery' schemes outside the English classroom, to 'guided reading' strategies, and many more besides that occur within our English lessons.

Reading strategies and skills

Reading in English is most typically divided into *fiction* and *non-fiction* reading. Many English departments approach their Key Stage 3 (KS3) curriculum by dividing schemes of learning into fiction and non-fiction strands. Schemes such as the study of a novel, or a varied collection of poems, would represent the study of fiction, whereas a non-fiction scheme may concentrate upon persuasive texts, such as a scheme on advertising or political speeches.

Other English departments approach the curriculum thematically. For example, a scheme of learning on 'War and words' may encompass war poetry, a novel such as Michael Morpurgo's brilliant *Private Peaceful*, first-person accounts of war, political speeches from the war, etc. These approaches have the benefit of creating a pattern of meaning, whereat students can connect vocabulary and ideas and build their knowledge and understanding.

What will be common across all schools is that the reading skills practised and honed by students will spiral upwards in terms of challenge and degree of difficulty. This will mean that many common reading strategies are revisited. This will complement the development of new, challenging vocabulary, ideas and knowledge. The following table includes a range of reading strategies to be taught in English.

Reading strategies	Definition
• Skimming	Reading quickly to get an overview of a text
• Scanning	Searching for the key information in a text
• Summarising	Synthesising the key ideas in a text
• Questioning	Formulating questions on a given text
• Inferring	Making meanings from clues given in a text
• Empathising	Reading 'between the lines' to find meaning in a text
• Visualising	Creating images to better understand a text
• Close reading	Homing in on key words or phrases
• Reading backwards and forwards	Being able to move around a text to clarify ideas and make connections
• Predicting	Making educated guesses

These reading strategies do need to be made explicit to students. If they understand the strategies they need to apply when reading, then they are better placed to read independently. Our ultimate aim is that students read fluently and independently, drawing upon these reading strategies automatically. As English teachers, we need to have an acute knowledge about where students are on the continuum between being *weak, dependent readers* and becoming *fluent, independent readers.*

There are many approaches to the teaching of reading to help develop vocabulary recognition and to develop reading skills. Crucially, creating a strong culture of reading in the classroom is key.

We need to question how we are going to foster reading for pleasure that complements the development of reading strategies. Reading will not flourish without being cultivated.

We must ask: Do we provide a range of reading materials that students can access? Are we talking about reading on a regular basis, celebrating and modelling the act of reading? Do students have a good knowledge of reading material that is well suited to them? Are our classrooms great adverts for reading: do we prove apt role models for reading?

Creating a thriving culture of reading doesn't stop in the English classroom, of course. Many schools undertake 'Big reads' or an annual 'Readathon'. They encourage regular author visits and make the library a learning hub of the school. Find out what your school does to promote reading and get involved.

Reading the 'literary canon'

The choice of reading material is often a battleground of debate. Such a debate could be simply mediated by agreeing that students need challenging texts, chosen by teachers, for their learning, alongside being guided to making their own choice of high-quality, wider reading.

English curriculum essentials

The 'literary canon' is lauded as central to the English curriculum. Since F. R. Leavis, in the 1950s, wrote the book *The Great Tradition*, effectively outlining an accepted 'canon' of great literature, debate as to who should be part of this 'great tradition' has been fought out tirelessly. His opening line states: 'The great English novelists are Jane Austen, George Eliot, Henry James, and Joseph Conrad – to stop for the moment at that comparatively safe point in history.'[1] Without doubt, any classification of quality is sure to arouse debate and criticism. Leavis had no intention of prescribing these novelists to an unwitting bunch of Year 7 English students, but it was the beginning of an important debate about what literature we should teach in English.

The debate shows no sign of slowing. Margaret Mathieson quoted Matthew Arnold in describing English teachers as 'The Preachers of Culture'. They were people on a mission to bring culture to the masses.

The question is: whose culture?

We must ask ourselves: Should our interests define what our students read? Should the interests of our students affect what we decide to read in the classroom? And whose 'canon' is it anyway?

Recently, many politicians and educationalists have undertaken the debate with thrusting arguments. The value of 'cultural capital' has become a clarion call for many. The idea is that the knowledge of prestigious and traditional literature provides a social value that can help with social mobility and becoming a success in life.

Although it is hard to argue with the value of the classics, such prescriptivism is likely to stick in the throat of many English teachers. In the most recent iterations of the National Curriculum, classics of the literary canon, such as the plays of Shakespeare and modern British fiction, have been cited as compulsory, with more specific recommendations, such as Romantic poetry and poetry of the First World War making the cut.

Few could argue with the ambition of such lists. Like going shopping, we need lists, otherwise we forget to buy the crucial ingredients we need – or even the healthy staples, milk and bread.

Not only that; there remains a great deal of choice for individual teachers, despite these prescribed lists.

In the reality of the classroom, a 'de facto canon' emerges, formed by the shared expertise of experienced English teachers. Ask English teachers what they teach and why, and the 'de facto canon' will become clear to you. Find out what students are reading. Find out what teachers are teaching successfully to the students in your school. Create your canon that is best suited for *your* students.

It is important to question your own knowledge of fiction for children. What have you read from Michael Morpurgo, Eoin Colfer, Frank Cottrell Boyce, Marcus Sedgewick, Meg Rosoff, Bali Rai and Alan Gibbons, etc.? What is popular and why? Many of these texts are future classics. The literary canon of tomorrow. We are the guardians and filters for such canon making.

Any public focus on the literary canon should not be seen as a rejection of modern texts at all, but instead a recognition that some literature does have greater prestige in our society. Death – in this instance – is paradoxically a good thing. When an author croaks it, their books take on a hallowed air. This vintage must of age often confers relic-like status onto prose and poetry that some then value more, like fine antiques.

In our role as English teachers, we can mediate that balance between students reading books of their own choosing, for their own pleasure, with our selection of challenging reading material (which we would hope also is a pleasure to read and experience). We need to select the best antiques and the best of modern fare. We can help by noting the rich and complex patterns that connect the two.

Michael Gove asked the following question in a speech at Brighton College: 'You come home to find your 17-year-old daughter engrossed in a book. Which would delight you more – if it were *Twilight* or *Middlemarch*?'

How do you respond? Is it a valid question?

As a father and English teacher, I find the question a difficult one.

First, I am happy that my daughter is reading. Too many teenagers have long since lost the pleasure of reading, or are snowed under by a dull, spirit-sapping exam regime. But I would undoubtedly *prefer* her to be reading *Middlemarch* if I was forced into a choice.

Perhaps the answer is achieved by not devising a false divide between the two novels; instead, we can recognise the value of *all* reading. We could encourage the wider reading of *Twilight* and place it in a rich Gothic tradition that encourages the reading of Bram Stoker, Mary Shelley and more.

It may be our place to lever more traditional reading into the diet of our students, but we should continue to encourage all reading of literature and celebrate it openly. We need to discuss less in terms of 'either/or' thinking, and instead more in terms of 'and/both' thinking when considering the canon and the what and how of teaching reading.

On Shakespeare

Almost all English teachers will likely have a largely positive opinion of reading and studying Shakespeare. The dense, challenging language was something you probably grew to appreciate, unpick and understand. Shakespeare, in many ways, may have marked us out as a success, as we mastered the complex challenge.

For many students, their experience is a negative one. It is characterised by struggle, misapprehension and bewilderment.

Few even canon-questioning teachers dispute the reading of Shakespeare at the core of what we learn in English. Sometimes greatness shines so brightly that disputing its value in a curriculum appears rather absurd. That being said, we should question the approach to teaching Shakespeare and seek to improve our practice.

I speak with English teachers who say that Shakespeare simply doesn't engage students. Yet, I know that many students in KS1 and KS2 undertake performances of Shakespeare and study the rich social context of the Elizabethan world with great success. Our question, then, should perhaps not be focused upon *what* is on the curriculum, but instead on the *how* of our teaching and learning approaches.

We should ask: What can we learn from the teaching of Shakespeare in primary school, or in drama classes? Knowledge of the language is essential, but we must remember that the plays were always meant to be interpreted in active and dynamic performances.

Too often, reading Shakespeare can be a slow, dry affair. It can be all metrical feet and language in translation, without the dynamism of debate and drama. It can elicit some scathing commentary from students. Arm yourself with an answer to the challenging question: 'Why are we studying this rubbish? It is too old!'

Of course, the best answer is to bring to life the raging jealousy of Othello, the scheming brilliance of Richard III and the lovesick impetuousness of Romeo with dramatic force. Teaching Shakespeare need not be dull, nor the language inaccessible.

Too often, teachers forget that Shakespeare is the most dramatic of affairs. Translating the language of the plays can be a lively and emotive experience, with group work, drama performance and debate being at the heart of understanding the themes, ideas and context of Shakespeare's plays. Move the desks in the classroom; travel to the drama studio; venture into the library to carry out research. Break the plays down into usable chunks and get students to grapple with the acts of translation and interpretation.

There are legions of resources and strategies to illuminate the study of Shakespeare. From shouting searing insults to debating fratricide and sexual identity (students always have a view on that!) – the opportunities for exciting learning are legion. See the section on **Pedagogy for teaching Shakespeare (and drama) in English**, in **Chapter 2**, for further ideas.

Undoubtedly, one of our crucial jobs as an English teacher is to unlock the magic and wisdom of Shakespeare and other great writers. We need to communicate that the challenge of accessing the sometimes archaic and difficult language has value for students.

We must, therefore, harness our passion for reading and literature, inspiring passion in our students. We must encourage reading for pleasure, while honing the reading skills of our students, so that they can tackle the challenge and rich complexities of the best that has been thought and written, from writers throughout history and into tomorrow.

Effective drama teaching

The teaching and learning of drama are important components in English. Too often drama is derided as play time. Used effectively, it can be a potent tool of critical analysis. It allows students to experience for themselves the physical and visual choices employed by dramatists. Acting can help students visualise and make physical complex concepts – making them tangible.

For some teachers, and indeed students, the idea of role play fills them with dread. The very wrong sort of dramatic tension is evoked. Many teachers are most confident teaching reading and writing, rather than drama or speaking and listening. Teachers must develop a drama repertoire that gives them confidence to employ such strategies in the classroom.

Drama is inextricably linked with speaking and listening pedagogy and performance. Drama activities, such as role play, can develop vital oracy skills for our students. For example, performing in role – perhaps the scripting and performance of an ironic take on the teacher–student relationship – can illuminate aspects of language such as *register* (the degree of formality in speech) and how power is conveyed through language.

Often, the very grammar of speech is only made truly comprehensible in performance. If students are studying a play text, they need to explore character through taking on the role of actor, or director, to help them make an informed interpretation. With activities such as '**character sculpting**', students can position characters in relation to one another; they can discuss and find evidence for body language, facial expressions and verbal expression. Students in the audience can perform as the '**choral voice**', determining the different critical perspectives on the action.

There is a rich range of play texts available for KS3, from classic novels, such as *Dracula*, converted to well-crafted play scripts, to instant modern classics, such as Morpurgo's *War Horse*, being readily available. At KS4, many staples have stood the test of time. *An Inspector Calls* is still engaging students with the 'trouble at t' mill', and the *Woman in Black* still has the power to scare. At KS5, bloody revenge tragedies such as *The Duchess of Malfi* sit alongside more modern classics such as *Oh, What a Lovely War!* or Bennett's hugely popular *The History Boys*.

You needn't leave the safety of the desk-filled classroom to invigorate a lesson with the spark of drama. By creating a '**forum theatre**', you can simply stop the action, and students can suggest alternative methods of performance or put forward different interpretations of the language. It is simply about creating an active culture of questioning: interrogating a play text. With any small-group drama, students can home in on specific extracts and give their own critical commentary that questions a text and prompts deep thinking about their reading.

There are some drama strategy stalwarts that have lasted in the crucible of the English classroom. Strategies such as '**hot seating**' allow students to explore a character from any text. Students can take on a character in role and be questioned while they attempt to remain in character. This is doubly useful, as the audience has to select thoughtful and apt questions, whereas the student in role needs to make lots of instantaneous decisions that can reveal a complex understanding of character worthy of exploration.

As we all too quickly realise, our role as an English teacher is a drama performance. It may lack the glamour of the West End stage, but our skills were honed in those confidence-building contributions we once made in the English classroom. The confidence gained in performing can be a boon in many immeasurable ways. We should, therefore, ensure that drama isn't an alien other in the English curriculum, scorned as a mere distraction. It is valuable.

You might just need some practice to build your own confidence. Seek out observations of drama experts in your school. Get yourself involved in drama workshops in your school and beyond. Also, no English teacher would feel complete without experiencing the inimitable theatre visit with a bunch of students who are determined to rustle sweet wrappers to a degree that would prompt Hamlet himself into swift retributive action!

If all of the world is a stage, then our students need some time treading the boards in the relative safety of the English classroom.

The power of poetry

Teaching poetry is a unique privilege. Poems are like polished diamonds: their compression of meaning and their beauty mean they are small but most often perfectly formed. This makes them ideal for the teaching parameters of an English lesson.

Only, akin to Shakespeare, not all students share this opinion. Poetry can receive a bad press from truculent teens. It can suffer from a bad reputation before a line is read. The reasons are complex, I'm sure. We need to focus upon reclaiming the reputation of poetry by teaching it brilliantly. Luckily, redemption is close at hand.

The very basis of poetry is music. Music, therefore, provides us with one of the keys for great teaching. How could we teach the complexities of poetry meter without borrowing a fleet of drums from the music department? How could we pass up the opportunity to compare poetry and song lyrics? By tapping into the interests and prior knowledge of our students, we can transform their perception of poetry as dry, dull and difficult.

The KS3 curriculum (and what comes before) should focus upon the rhythms of poetry. It should also not shy away from unveiling the complex layers of language inherent in all great poetry. Students need to read and write with a focus upon the figurative language that has become synonymous with poetry from Homer to Hughes: similes, metaphors, personification and hyperbole, etc.

A great modern poem, which serves as a metaphor for poetry itself is, is Carol Ann Duffy's 'Valentine'. It is an original take on the love poem, offering the lover a gift of an onion. This extended metaphor provides us with an apt symbol for poetry. Students must peel back the layers of meaning. They need to struggle with the language (weeping optional) in a rewarding search for meaning. We are integral to making that struggle worthwhile.

Most great poetry captures emotion at its core. If we can connect the music and the emotion, we may help our students capture the diamond beauty of poetry.

Wordsworth famously wrote, in his Preface to his *Lyrical Ballads*, that poetry was the 'spontaneous overflow of powerful feelings'. We must remember that these fragments of emotion may stay with our students for a lifetime. We don't just teach poetry for the limits of an examination. Poetry can prove a timely reminder of this truth.

Some great poetry has stood the test of time and the blunt attacks of a disinterested few. For example, Andrew Marvell's 'To his coy mistress' still has the power to charm and shock as if it were written yesterday. William Blake's 'London' can convey with brute force the stark inequality faced by children in the world. Auden's 'Nightmail' has the power to stir students into a distant past with its charging rhythms. The list, and the beat, goes on.

What would be on your list? What poets and poems would best evoke the powerful feelings of our students?

See the section on **Pedagogy for teaching poetry**, in **Chapter 2**, for teaching and learning ideas.

Effective teaching of writing

A good writer is typically someone who reads a lot. There is an inextricable link between skilful readers and successful writers. The more a child reads, the more they become aware of the many codes and conventions that comprise different genres and text types.

Therefore, the modelling of good writing is crucial to the effective teaching of writing. Reading lots of examples based upon a given genre or text type establishes the foundations for students to build their own writing. Essentially, our students pass through different stages in their writing development. These include three broad areas:

- **Imitation**: Students take years to internalise generic patterns and conventions. *Once upon a time* they learn these by imitating narratives and text structures. Ask a young child in a primary school to write a story, and they will probably furnish you with a good working fairytale that ends with 'The end'.

- **Elaboration**: Students then develop upon the generic patterns and structures they have borrowed with their own unique ideas. This may include creating a hybrid text, such as a fairytale blended with the unique vocabulary choices and narrative techniques that they have been developing daily.

- **Reinvention**: This latter stage reflects when students are able to devise text types and narratives almost wholly independently. They may create *hybrid* narratives – such as a *dystopian romance*, etc.

Each of these stages will be reflected in our individual students. Each individual will be at a different point of development. What is clear is that we have an undertaking to move students from being *dependent* upon our input (such as providing writing frames that structure their writing, or providing models of great writing from which they can borrow ideas, vocabulary, etc.) to becoming *interdependent*: that is to say, ready to confidently elaborate upon the structural supports we provide.

At the imitation stage, students are reliant upon the teacher to model the entire writing process. This stage isn't simply for primary school children – it is characteristic of many of our KS3 students. We need to make explicit each step of effective writing: ideas generation, planning, drafting, sharing, evaluating, proofreading and revising their writing. We need to repeat the process until it becomes something like automatic – like driving a car (not the students, that isn't legal).

Novice writers need to repeatedly practise writing in different genres and for different purposes. They need to have a certain grasp of what writing to 'describe', 'analyse', 'inform', 'narrate' and 'persuade' means and what techniques to employ for that purpose. They also need to practise writing for different audiences, thereby learning to adapt their language and their level of formality – or their *register*. It is a simple case of what Doug Lemov called 'practice makes permanent'.[2]

Activities such as *shared writing* – where the teacher leads the writing with the whole class, asking students to contribute with ideas to substitute, delete, switch and improve upon sentences and vocabulary choices – help students to create a mental template for their own writing.

The final stage is *independent writing*, which is the ultimate goal for our students. We want them to be able to respond to any given exam question, or real-world writing task, with automatic understanding of the style, language choices and structures required to communicate effectively and fluently. This, of course, takes many repeated opportunities to write and receive feedback. For the effective teaching of writing, we need to repeatedly loop the development process, providing timely and appropriate teaching support.

We are what we repeatedly do. Students' writing becomes what they repeatedly practise.

Planning, drafting and proofreading

Another aspect of writing we want students to complete automatically is the ability to plan, draft and proofread their own writing with success. You would be forgiven for thinking that, to some students, these three skills are alien. But, as F. Scott Fitzgerald stated about the process of writing: 'Nothing any good isn't hard'.

Most students naturally enjoy the spark of imagination needed for the act of writing. The immediate gratification of writing can have a palpable, positive effect. You may remember being wholly lost in the world of writing during your experience at school. The processes of planning, drafting and proofreading, in contrast, lack immediacy and often lack pleasure, and therefore students often fail to perceive their true value. We must make their value explicit. We must also drill away at these processes to ensure they become something like automatic for our students.

The crafting and drafting of writing often work best with lots of feedback given on students' writing. By making their working process clear to them (such as reading their writing aloud), you can unpick the importance of drafting improvements and eliminating errors. You can explain to them how making small improvements can save lives. Sentences such as 'Let's eat, Grandma!' are far more effective than the clarion call for cannibalism unwittingly made in the sentence 'Let's eat Grandma!'

Resources that scaffold such writing processes, such as 'planning frames' (for instance, providing step-by-step boxes for each paragraph in order) or 'literacy mats' (a helpful collection of grammar pointers, spelling tips and more), are helpful in making these skills easier to apply when writing.

In **Chapter 5**, **Differentiation in English**, there are lots of helpful tips on how you can specifically help individual writers. Repeated often enough, these crucial aspects of writing do become automatic for most students. When students perceive they are improving their writing, they invariably begin to enjoy the gritty process of honing their writing.

If we raise the standard of expectation within the minds of our students, then we can improve their writing. How do teachers do this effectively? Making their writing processes visible, celebrating successes, providing exemplar models of student writing and providing lots of time to respond to feedback are crucial in driving improvements in their writing. Oh, and lots of reading and talking about writing.

Effective teaching of spelling, punctuation and grammar (SPaG)

The 'how we were taught' debate often rages around grammar, and every generation appears to have a different narrative. The most experienced teachers among us often speak of being taught grammar by rote learning, whereas younger teachers often explain that their learning of grammar, at least what they remember, was *tacit learning*, that is a learning by a sort of osmosis. Some people were taught by rote, drilled into learning the rules of grammar, before they were allowed to pursue more interesting writing activities.

It is valuable to know what has come before for our students. They are taught much about grammar before they ever reach secondary school. My experience is that many primary schools foreground much of the *metalanguage* (the fancy labels we use, such as modifiers or noun phrases) associated with grammar with great skill. Students become well versed in its uses.

That being said, when they arrive at secondary school, much of their knowledge isn't fully committed to their working memory. Perhaps it is a difficulty issue, or the fact that spelling and grammar lack the emotional associations required for deep learning. It is just plain dull. Maybe it is the fact that some teachers lack confidence in teaching grammar well and habitually.

Debra Myhill has coordinated the undertaking of much research into the teaching of grammar. Her work has shown evidence that teaching grammar in context (that is to say, as part of the study of a text type or a specific genre) is the most successful method of teaching grammar. She also makes the claim that this grammar teaching in the context of reading and approaching different genres of writing is best for the most able writers.

In contrast, Daisy Christodoulou, of The Curriculum Centre, argues that many more hours of explicit grammar instruction are required to help students have the ability to really grasp grammar, before tackling other important aspects, such as writing for a specific audience and purpose. Read Daisy's short case study here:

CASE STUDY: GRAMMAR AND THE CURRICULUM CENTRE

Teaching grammar out of context is often criticised. And indeed, it may well be true that in the 1950s teachers spent too much time getting pupils to learn abstract grammatical rules and not enough time thinking about how to apply those rules in their writing.

However, what we know about the limitations of working memory suggests that a decontextualised approach might have some strengths. Lots of grammatical rules are complex and difficult to understand. Too often, a contextualised approach seems to mean teaching grammatical rules at the same time as teaching something else – for example, teaching adjectives in a unit on creative writing, or the apostrophe in a unit on persuasive writing. The problem with this approach is that it has the potential to overwhelm working memory. The other problem is that it distorts the internal logic of grammar. Pupils learn about adjectives even if they haven't done nouns, or they learn about apostrophes even though they haven't done pronouns.

The Curriculum Centre's approach is to have one discrete grammar lesson a week where pupils focus on nothing but a particular grammatical concept or rule. These concepts are sequenced logically: nouns before adjectives, parts of speech before sentence structures, simple sentences before complex sentences. Once pupils have learned a concept or rule, the teacher can refer to it in all their other lessons and in the comments and targets they give on written work. The writing assessment rubric that is used for all writing in all subjects refers to the language and concepts pupils have learned in grammar.

This approach requires pupils to apply their grammatical knowledge, but it ensures that the grammatical knowledge base is firmly in place in advance of application. It gives pupils the time they need to master grammar, rather than assuming they will be able to 'pick it up' in context. Then they can apply it in the contexts of their own writing.

Daisy Christodoulou, Research and Development Manager at ARK and former English teacher

You may be worried that such experts have delivered the solution and you are still scrambling about making sense of the problem. Don't worry – the teaching of grammar is an area of uncertainty for most teachers. Sometimes, you learn alongside your students.

Think of the problem more simply. First, explore what the common SPaG errors students make are, and what solutions teachers typically employ. The following table is a simple guide to such problems and their solutions.

Problem	Solution
• **Handwriting is clumsy or not fully legible**	Often deemed an issue for primary school teachers, many teachers face this issue. Tackle potentially simple answers. Are they rushing? Are they using poor equipment? Are they applying too much or too little pressure?
	Some students with spelling issues or gaps in their understanding can write illegibly to mask their issues. Check for related causes.
	Ask students to leave lines between their writing to encourage a more careful application of their handwriting.
	Identify any specific patterns to remedy. Do they apply unnecessary capital letters

out of habit? Do *g* and *y* rest on the line properly? Does *f* go below the line fully?

Do students lack skills in cursive writing? This handwriting style encourages students to think in terms of letter clusters – often having a positive impact upon their spelling.

- **Spelling errors** Are there common errors, or is it just a symptom of rushing or poor proofreading habits? You will quickly note common issues, such as homonyms (e.g. there, they're and their) or words with tricky vowel clusters or silent letters.

  A recap of common issues, such as tense or specific *-ed* verb ending errors can be addressed in individual feedback or as a group.

  There are some long-standing spelling strategies you can train students to use:

  1 Start segmenting words, focusing upon tricky phonemic patterns, such as '*gh*' suffixes or vowel clusters such as '*ea*'.

  2 Create little rules or mnemonics to help students remember spellings, e.g. Fri*ends* always stick to the *end*.

  3 Learn a spelling through the classic '*look, cover, write and check*' method.

  4 Encourage students to consider similar words that share similar root spellings.

  Of course, don't forget the humble dictionary. Students need training in using a dictionary, but the rewards are huge. Encourage dictionary games and word hunts to enliven the process.

Create specific spelling banks. If you are teaching a novel, identify complex spellings beforehand and anticipate common errors. Display challenging vocabulary and get students to use the words repeatedly.

- **Punctuation errors**

There are common patterns of punctuation issues that beguile students. These will likely need addressing in repeated cycles over time. Issues such as the punctuation of speech typically trouble students. Experienced teachers also recognise patterns. For example, confident semicolon usage will almost certainly require repeated and explicit teaching.

Encourage self-correction with each complete sentence they write.

A common issue is a weakness with demarcating sentences. Rules for using commas successfully are worth repeated practising. Teach the use of a comma explicitly, such as placing commas before a conjunction, or after an adverbial sentence starter, etc.

Get students to correct unpunctuated writing of their own or a model.

As with most writing, get students to read their writing aloud and trace their punctuation use alongside their expression. Question marks and exclamation marks often become evident to students in their reading.

- **Little variety of punctuation**

Get students to read their work aloud, considering the pace and effect created by their punctuation use.

21

Have a simple punctuation diagram above their writing to use as a checklist.

Use writing models that exemplify a range of punctuation. Explore punctuation common to genres, such as the ellipsis in mystery writing.

- **Incomplete sentences or awkward syntax**

Students need to understand the basic ingredients of a sentence and the different sentence types: simple, complex and compound. Drilling in specific rules eliminates the most common errors over time. Get them verb hunting and play repeatedly with examples.

Shared writing with other students often initiates a critical dialogue where two minds can battle with the fluency of the writing.

Get students to physically act out the use of different word groups in the different parts of the sentence. This illuminates typical patterns of syntax and its flexibility.

- **Little variety in sentence structures**

Students will often default to basic sentences that follow the 'subject, verb, object' pattern. They can practise using a range of sentence starters that encourage variety, such as beginning with an adverb, e.g. 'Strangely, she left the train . . .', followed by an adjective, e.g. 'Golden skies drifted overhead'.

Explicitly teach students to employ a breadth of discourse markers.

Give students simple sentence structures and get them to elaborate upon the sentence structure for effect.

Play grammar games where they have to
employ different sentence types.

Speaking and listening in English

Oracy has always been the poor sibling to reading and writing. Great
English teachers recognise the crucial importance of oracy. As
explored in the previous section on SPaG, reading aloud and talking
through their writing are primary strategies for encouraging
accurate writing. The importance of speaking and listening cannot
be underestimated. This means we must place debate, dialogue and
drama at the core of our pedagogy.

Even a rudimentary understanding of child language acquisition
will spell out that oracy provides the very foundation for successful
reading and writing. I know, for example, that my young daughter's
oral proficiency will correlate strongly with her future ability to read
and write successfully. Indeed, reading itself is a form of listening
– described here by E. D. Hirsch:

> Reading – even skimming – is indeed accompanied by
> 'subvocalization'. Although some teachers use this term to refer
> to children whispering to themselves as they make the
> transition from reading out loud to silent reading, researchers
> use this term to refer to the internal voice we all hear while we
> read silently. We use an inner voice and an inner ear. Reading
> IS listening.[3]

The teaching of oracy does span across the curriculum beyond
English, but it has a central place in our practice. Talk often
illuminates the difficult processes of reading and writing for
students. Practising what they write through oral rehearsal has an
important role in enhancing the quality of students' writing. The
opposite is also true.

Often, the higher degree of formality inherent in writing can
improve the quality of their talk and their act of speaking. Simply
writing a script can help improve the standard of students' talk,

giving it structure and helping students consider their language choices more thoughtfully. By listening to the teacher modelling talk and reading, students better develop their comprehension of complex vocabulary and their understanding of differing registers, etc.

We need to scaffold their language to ensure they can understand how and when to adapt their spoken language to suit the occasion.

We may debate about who sets the standard for 'standard English', but we all recognise that students having the capacity to adapt and control their language is a key to future success.

All language and communication are essentially social. We need to harness this dynamic aspect of language. In English, we need to invest time and effort to elevate the status of oracy and provide more formal opportunities for talk rooted in our practice on a regular basis.

Sometimes, English teaching is at the mercy of preparing for high-stakes examinations. We must revisit the skills and knowledge that will make our students confident learners in a changing world. A capacity to speak eloquently and adapt their talk in a whole host of contexts will see our students flourish beyond the exam hall. We must, therefore, raise the status of speaking and listening and ensure they are at the core of English teaching and learning.

New teachers can fear student talk driving learning, as there can be a sense of giving up control of behaviour, or lacking order in the classroom. Rather than avoid talk, discussion and debate, we must ensure we structure talk with clear parameters of behaviour and the highest of expectations. As with most things, it is about balance. For a group activity, ensure timing is explicit, roles are clear and outcomes are clear too. With these foundations in place, speaking and listening can flourish.

Harnessing the power of technology

Technology is only a tool. It is a tool that will not *fix* the teaching of English, nor be a magic elixir that makes teachers great; however, it can help enhance the skills we seek to develop in English: reading, writing and speaking and listening. We should look to utilise it for our benefit.

Our very idea of a 'text' has now become something that is often *multimodal*. Texts that include a complex synthesis of conventional language, images, sound, hyperlinks, etc. are now the norm.

According to research from the National Literacy Trust, '63.8 per cent read using a computer and 55.9 per cent read on their mobile phone. 20.4 per cent of young people say that they read using an iPad, while 21.1 per cent read using other electronic devices.'[4] Technology is shaping how children read and receive language. Students habitually read web pages that encompass traditional reading content and images and film connected with a succession of hyperlinks.

The typical experience for the audience of this book using technology in their schooling may be characterised by frustration and limitation. You may be picturing an ICT room with row upon row of lumbering computer terminals. Between traipsing to the computer room, a unique and mysterious event, starting the machine and waiting for the teacher to work out the mysteries of this new setting, half the time you had to learn was already lost.

Still, many teachers experience the frustrations of booking computer rooms or bumping up against impractical barriers such as school Internet security settings. However, the tide is turning. In many schools, using technology as a tool for learning in English is becoming more frequent, more familiar and more flexible.

With the advent of tablet technology, the annual pilgrimage to the computer room is becoming a thing of the past. The technology can come to the classroom. With such devices, a new vista of tools for learning is emerging. A tablet device becomes a tool for research, a video camera to record speaking and listening activities, a visualiser to instantly display models of students' ongoing writing, an annotation tool, etc.

In any one given lesson, students can research a topic or watch a pre-prepared presentation, before saving and using such information in applications to create their own presentations. They can record ideas and discussion or drama performances, before showing them back to the class and receiving feedback.

That being said, you can become an inspirational teacher of English without a reliance on technology. The opportunities provided by using technological tools can be tremendous. What is crucial to recognise is that great teaching begins with great pedagogy – not the tools of technology.

We must begin with devising strategies for how our students will best learn the knowledge and skills they need in English. If technological tools can enhance our core pedagogy, such as giving feedback and improving note-taking, or the quality of discussion and debate, then we should seek to exploit those tools.

As English teachers, we must be wary of simply using Google as a proxy for high-quality teacher instruction. Students need to be trained in researching using the Internet. They need training in using various mobile technology applications successfully. The time and investment need to be carefully planned, but, with well-guided use, these are valuable tools for learning.

Technology and the influence of new media are often easy targets for blame for a decline in the English language, rather than constructive tools for learning. No doubt, the impact of television has affected the reading habits of children, but, rather than attempting to turn back the tide like King Canute, we must harness the possibilities of technology and new media communication.

For example, we can teach the poetry of *Beowulf* by utilising the modern animated fantasy film (which sees Ray Winstone bring his angry cockney tones to the Anglo-Saxon myth) as a tool to increase understanding. In fact, we can draw upon a smorgasbord of modern monsters to illuminate the mythic beast – from Godzilla to Jaws. We can draw students in with their prior cultural knowledge, thereby helping them understand the relevance of the ancient story, before beguiling them with the music of the poetry.

The power of real audiences

The use of technology and the Internet has opened up education to the transformative power of real audiences. When students write a blog or a website, or share a YouTube video, their intrinsic motivation can skyrocket. Students can begin to see the true value of crafting and drafting their writing, if they know that a real audience will receive and interact with their efforts.

Some of the most powerful writing my students have ever produced has been *real*: letters to authors, a letter to David Cameron (defending the youth of today from being blamed for 'broken Britain'), or producing creative writing for local websites.

 With the advent of blog platforms such as **Blogger** and **Word-Press**, English teachers are able to create instant websites to share research, to communicate between groups and to present real writing. Websites such as **www.padlet.com** can be eminently useful for creating an online space for interactive discussion and a collaborative research space, whereas other sites, such as **www.tagxedo.com**, can help you and your students create word clouds that are the stimulus for close language analysis. With **Google Docs,** we are able to create online documents that can be shared, edited and co-constructed to make the writing process interactive and collaborative.

The opportunities are limitless and flexible. To use technology in English effectively does take teacher training and no little practice, but we should explore the ever-developing opportunities provided by technological tools and platforms.

Many new teachers are far more confident with technology than the generation of teachers that preceded them. Yet, you should not be alarmed if your idea of technology enhancing reading is turning off your alarm clock as you read in bed. Many more important skills need to be mastered by the novice teacher before you begin experimenting with technology apps, etc.

Judge your own technological proficiency and look to develop your knowledge and skill step by step. Mastering PowerPoint and a few other simple tools will go a long way to providing the essential tools you need for your initial trembling steps into teaching.

Some teachers are busy forging ahead with technological expertise for our benefit. Christopher Waugh, at the Nautical School in London, has every English student producing their writing, not in conventional exercise books, but in an online blog, creating a platform for timely feedback and a global audience. See his case study here:

CASE STUDY: BLOGGING IN ENGLISH

There is a lot said about 'twenty-first-century skills' and the apparent need for schools to engage with the new inventions of the modern world. Both sides of this argument are compelling. On one hand, the fundamental knowledge and skills that are taught in schools have barely changed in the last 150 years, and the established methods of developing these that have been honed and crafted over that time should be abandoned at our peril; on the other hand, the world is changing fast, and the skills and attributes that will ensure success in the twenty-first century are not the same as those of the people whom our education system was created to serve.

The resolution to this may come through defying this apparent dichotomy. Blogging is an excellent example of this. Rather than it being a 'revolutionary, new' means of communication, educationalists can – with a slight alteration in their mindset – use blogging as a means of amplifying everything we already know works about learning in schools.

To illuminate this point, here are some examples from a classroom where students and I have eschewed our books for blogs:

- All the materials, resources, scrawls on the board, student exemplars and references from our learning programme go into the teacher's blog. This is freely accessible online by the students and their families. Everyone has access to everything all the time, and can subscribe so any new material is automatically posted to them. They can also ask questions and add their own material at the touch of a button.

- The students have their own blogs, in which they keep everything they write and create throughout the year. They, and the wider world, are free to access and respond to each other's work and they make the decision about when they believe their draft work is ready to publish to the world.

- Feedback to students is achieved via the commenting mechanism and occurs at the time the students need it – while they are doing the work, as opposed to after it is completed. A dialogue is generated in the comments section of their blogs, where the students respond to the feedback and ask further questions.

In the end, the students in these classes are being exposed to the same content and developing the same skills as anyone else learning English in England might – the difference is that the mode of interaction is transformed by being more immediate, specific and interactive. The teacher takes the role of editor and collaborator, assisting the students to craft and improve their work before it goes out into the world – just as it has always been.

**Christopher Waugh, Subject Leader of English
and founder of 'Edutronic'**

I would take inspiration from Chris and his fantastic online facility for writing and English study, with the safe knowledge that such practice isn't yet widespread. Perhaps you could be another such pioneer who harnesses technology to enhance English? Maybe it is a new method of teaching the English curriculum that you can get your teeth into, when you have established yourself in the classroom?

TALKING POINTS

- Based on your own prior knowledge, what areas of the curriculum would you consider your strengths and weaknesses? What next steps do you need to make to improve your knowledge?
- How much do you know about the National Curriculum for English and the curriculum in your school? Does this knowledge shape your views of topics discussed in this chapter?
- How will you balance the functional literacy required of English language, with a passion and interest for literature needed for a study of English literature? How will the two aspects overlap and reinforce one another?

Notes

1 Leavis, F. R. (2008) *The Great Tradition*, London: Faber & Faber, p. 1.
2 Lemov, D. (2012) *Practice Perfect: 42 Rules for Getting Better at Getting Better*, San Francisco, CA: Jossey-Bass.
3 E. D. Hirsch; see http://blog.coreknowledge.org/2013/01/31/why-is-there-so-much-listening-in-the-core-knowledges-reading-program/
4 This can be found on the website for The National Literacy Trust (2012) 'Children's Reading Today'; see www.literacytrust.org.uk/assets/0001/4450/Young_people_s_reading_-_FINAL_REPORT.pdf

2 Pedagogy essentials for great English lessons

Almost every new teacher has two key priorities. First, with some trepidation, is the question, 'How do I get them to behave?' Second, it comes to the crucial question: 'What teaching strategies will work?' Great English teachers develop an arsenal of flexible approaches for almost every eventuality.

 New teachers should plunder every possible resource. Websites such as **TES Resources** (www.tes.co.uk/teaching-resources) can complement a range of great books to buy and the schemes of learning already established in your school to help build your repertoire of teaching and learning strategies. This chapter will hopefully provide you with a great starting point for such a required repertoire of pedagogy.

There are many theories that propound different methods of instruction, from more *constructivist* approaches, with teaching and learning based around purposeful social interaction, to methods considered more traditional, such as '*direct instruction*', which is a specific approach to sequenced steps of demonstration, modelling and guided practice.

New approaches to pedagogy include '*project-based learning*', the '*co-construction*' of learning with students and the '*flipped learning*' model, where students utilise technology to learn new knowledge, through different media, before then developing their under-standing in lesson time. A quick web search of any of these terms will give you a wealth of useful information. Then, crucially, work out which strategies will work best for your students in your school context.

These approaches are, of course, always reliant upon the core foundations of all pedagogy: effective teacher explanations, rigorous questioning and debate, with modelling to guide the understanding of students. Concentrate upon these, and any innovations you apply, such as technology, will be rooted in solid ground.

Like most things in life, balance and variety are key. Students need expert teacher instruction. They need to build note-making skills and they need explicit modelling of both successful reading and writing. Once they have developed relative expertise, we then need to employ strategies to encourage independence and critical thinking.

There is no definitive teaching method. There is no silver bullet strategy. There is a lot of trial and error in your context for your unique classes. There are, however, simple guiding principles underlying great pedagogy, in English and across the curriculum.

A key question is: 'Is the pedagogy challenging students appropriately?' Is the pedagogy in what Lev Vygotsky defined as students' *'zone of proximal development'* (ZPD). That is to say, is it challenging enough to engage students, but not so challenging that it makes students give up? Like Goldilock's porridge, in difficulty terms, aim for 'not too easy, but not too hard'.

Pedagogy for great writing

Great writing is our core business. Whether it is a suspenseful piece of narrative or an attention-stealing speech, we need to ensure students successfully understand a range of written genres. They need to become familiar with the generic conventions of any given genre, beginning with imitation and moving to independent expertise.

Scaffolding your students' understanding is essential: using clear explanations, oral rehearsal and utilising models of great writing are our core methods for success. We should aim to stimulate the prior knowledge of our students and support them through developing their own writing style.

Oral rehearsal

A crucial way to activate the important prior knowledge of students, based on the many texts they have already read and written, is to promote discussion of the topic or genre at hand.

For example, if they were writing a book review, we would expect they have read some reviews before. Read some reviews to one another and talk about them. We can activate this knowledge so that they apply it to their current writing.

If they are writing about a topic, such as war, then students can reactivate their existing vocabulary related to the subject of war. A quick mind map of ideas and terms, shared and discussed among the group, can provide students with the requisite prior knowledge to begin writing with confidence. There is gold to be mined in these tangential discussions. We must, therefore, allocate time for discussion and provide opportunities for students to talk about their existing knowledge.

Modelling

Modelling is arguably the most important teaching strategy in the English teacher's repertoire. It is essential. All successful writers have a clear sense of the conventions of their given genre. Great writers match or often challenge such conventions, blending the conventions of different genres adeptly. It is obvious that, if students are to write a Gothic narrative, then they need to read and engage with a range of Gothic texts – novels or extracts from novels, short stories, poems or relevant media texts. Here are some useful strategies for modelling:

- **Close reading**: Show an extract and closely analyse it for generic conventions, language devices employed, etc. You can model *text marking* – the process of making concise notes on a given text. You can lead this, or students can work in small groups, once you have clearly established how they should go about their text marking.

- **Sequencing**: Students can be given a text reduced to shorter extracts, out of sequence. This has the benefit of having students consider conventional generic structures. By quickly cutting up a model, you can get them to reflect upon the development of their own writing, while honing their sense of the generic writing structure.

- **Multiple models**: Select a range of models, such as a series of given extracts of dystopian fiction, for example. Students can individually or collaboratively compare and contrast, classify, close read and text mark, or rank by effectiveness.

- **Jigsaw modelling**: Have different groups study individual models and then have an *expert* circulate the key information to other groups.

- **Graded modelling**: As Vygotsky's ZPD identified, students work best with accessible models relative to their current ability. With this in mind, show them models that are one level above their current attainment. You can create groups within a class in this manner, which is great for differentiation.

- **Model phrases**: All genres of writing have their own typical phrases and sentence openers. For example, identify the analytical or comparative phrases required for essay writing, such as 'On the contrary . . .', 'Likewise, . . .' and 'Conversely, . . .', and give students a glossary to get them started.

Making models

After the analysis of effective models, students need to imitate and play with these models. This can be done in a variety of ways:

- **Shared writing**: A really high-impact strategy involving the teacher leading a given piece of writing. The teacher leads the writing, questioning students so that they contribute appropriately. This is a powerful strategy for modelling excellence, allowing the teacher to differentiate questions to include everyone in the crucial decisions every successful writer undertakes when they write. It can positively model how every writer drafts: making errors, substitutions and improvements as they write. Just ensure you set clear boundaries for oral contributions.

- **Teacher modelling**: If you try writing what the students are tasked with writing yourself, you become the ultimate role model. This method not only establishes a sense of trust, with some lively opportunities for some shared camaraderie, but it can illuminate for you, and them, the difficulties and opportunities the students face in their writing. Not only that, you have a ready-made exemplar. It is also fun!

- **'Flip and reverse'**: Given a model starter to any given piece of writing, students are asked to play with the conventions of the writing. They may continue in the given style, or *reverse* the style of the starter extract. They could *flip* the argument, or even the genre conventions you would expect to be employed. If a student can begin to play games with generic conventions, then they clearly can understand the nuances of the given genre.

- **Collaborative writing**: Students are asked to create a model, but they have to write it together. They can write alternate sentences, or one student can source great vocabulary choices from a thesaurus, or research the topic at hand, while their partner writes. This allows for lots of constructive discussion and oral rehearsal.

Micro-writing

We most often wish to build writing skills by having students practise elements of a given genre. By undertaking really short *micro-writing*, students can experiment with their writing and have a really specific focus upon their vocabulary choices and the grammatical constructions they are deploying. Here are some ideas (these double as great writing starters):

- **Six-word film plots**: Made popular by a passing Internet fad, this simple compression of an entire narrative into only six words really challenges students to find the core message of a given narrative. Try it yourself! My attempt would be the film *Gladiator*: **A swords and sandals gladiatorial gore-fest!**

- **Seven-word biographies**: Another fun, genre-focused writing activity. You can see the opportunities are endless in terms of selecting genres and text types! Here is my effort based on the Bard: **Domed genius. Changed the writing world forever.**

- **Ten-word tall tales**: You get the idea! Try your own. Give students rules and structures that add challenge, such as asking them to include four types of punctuation, etc.

- **Haiku and tenko poems**: These compressed poems get students selecting vocabulary and organising sentence structures with real precision and focus.

- **Mobile phone number narratives**: Get students to use their mobile phone numbers to create a structure for sentence lengths; e.g., for the number seven, they need to include a seven-word sentence, etc. It really concentrates their mind on crafting sentence structures.

- **Uplevelling**: Give students individual sentences that they need to improve. They could be given specific instructions, e.g., 'Use an adverb sentence starter', etc.

Improving writing accuracy

It is essential that students develop good habits of written accuracy and develop a systematic approach to proofreading. You must give students the time and support structures necessary to reflect on the accuracy and success of their writing.

- **Self-reflection time**: Specially allocate time for students to review, reread and draft their writing. You may wish to scaffold this with resources, such as *literacy mats*, accessible dictionaries, etc. Some students will need to home in on one area to allow them to do it effectively. Jackie Beere labelled this **DIRT** (dedicated improvement and reflection time).

- **Peer proofreading**: Given clear parameters for making supportive and constructive comments, students often enjoy proofreading the work of others rather than their own. It can stimulate effective dialogue about improvements. They will need guidance about what to look for and how to feed back to their peers. Model this fully, and they can flourish.

- **Peer critique**: Originated by the brilliant **Ron Berger** (I strongly encourage you to read his book, *The Ethic of Excellence*, and type in 'Austin's Butterfly' into **YouTube** and watch a powerful example of critique), this method of peer feedback sets up student work in a gallery format, with students giving *'kind, helpful and specific'* feedback. By using post-it notes, students can get really useful feedback on their writing.

Engaging grammar strategies

The teaching of grammar is an area where English teachers feel less secure. As with most aspects of English, it is about building student confidence through repetition and practice. Such practice does not need to be stiflingly dull. Here are some lively approaches that show SPaG can be taught be taught meaningfully and memorably.

- **Practice drills**: There are many resources out there to help students drill crucial grammar skills. Great websites, such as **www.chompchomp.com**, can provide a ready-made resource for students' practice of important aspects of their grammar and written accuracy.

- **Create a language**: This strategy works for fresh-faced Year 7 students, all the way up to KS5 English language students.

Rather than teach word classes as atomised and inert objects, get students to analyse the very roots of language by creating their own. Start with word classes and basic functions, before exploring common prefixes and suffixes. You can move on to syntax and sentence types and structures. The options are endless. 'Jabberwocky' is a good starting point. This activity can be as short or as long as you like. The level of challenge is also easily adaptable for any group.

- **Spelling bee**: Transform the humble spelling test into a lively competition akin to the American national competition. Websites and competitions, including *The Times* **Spelling Bee**, have become very popular, and any teacher can create their own model, as an individual or team game. It is a great way to place common misspellings, such as *rhythm, necessary* or *technique*, in a purposeful context. You can have rounds on subject-specific language, such as poetic terminology or *homophones*, etc.

- **Connect a clause**: Cut up some complex sentence structures and get students to play with different variations on sentence structures. It can help support students to enlarge their variety of sentences structures. You can enlarge them and discuss choices with the whole class, with different students holding the clause and being shifted accordingly.

- **Sentence starters**: As a quick lesson starter, provide a range of optional sentence starters that exhibit different ways to open a sentence, such as with an adverb or an adjective, rather than relying upon pronouns such as 'I' or the definite ('the') and indefinite ('a') articles. It is also a good way to explore the active and passive voices and the different effects they can create.

- **Grammar mnemonics**: You can use, or indeed create with students, memorable mnemonics to help students embed common grammatical rules or terms. These are common in primary schools, so aim to find out what your students already know. Examples include **FANBOYS** for coordinating conjunctions (for, and, nor, but, or, yet, so). You can create one with students for common word groups or useful discourse markers, etc.

- **Adverbial charades**: Using adverbs as a sentence starter opens up all sorts of opportunities for plain, interesting fun! A student moves in the fashion of the adverb, prompting the audience to make educated guesses. The range and breadth of answers stimulate some great writing. Of course, this method is applicable to *verbs* and *adjectives* just as effectively.

Pedagogy for great reading

The pleasure we have gained from reading is often cited as one of the main reasons we decided to teach English. We should unashamedly flaunt our passion for reading.

We should read to students. We should read with students. We should talk about what we are reading. We should get students talking to one another about what they enjoy reading.

Inspiring an enthusiasm for reading can be one of the singularly greatest gifts we can confer upon our students. We must seek to expand the reading horizons of our students. By developing their reading skills, they are more likely to read further – a virtuous circle.

We should aim to develop **pre-reading** strategies to build solid foundations, **mid-reading** strategies to reinforce understanding and **post-reading** strategies to consolidate their understanding.

Pre-reading strategies

- **Word clouds**: Create words clouds (websites such as **http:// padlet.com** do this easily) based on vocabulary that illuminates a given topic, genre or narrative. Get students discussing these vocabulary choices, activating their prior knowledge, while interrogating a writer's vocabulary choices.

- **Twenty questions**: Get students to devise as many questions as they can for a given topic or text. For example, get students to read a blurb or view a front cover of a novel or images related to a topic or theme.

- **Image gallery**: Create an image gallery that includes symbols and images related to a given text. Get students to discuss recognisable patterns, ideas or any generic features.

- **Research**: Get students to actively research a given genre, author, historical context, etc.

- **Vocabulary games**: There are many fun, competitive games you can play with a dictionary or any given page of a text, such as getting students to hunt down specific words, etc. Websites, such as **www.knoword.org**, provide some lively ready-made games.

Mid-reading strategies

- **Meaning moles**: Have students researching away on key word definitions or researching topics (if you have access to tablet technologies, this becomes incredibly easy, or use the humble dictionary) as you read.

- **Word hunting**: You can help students record interesting vocabulary choices, for further discussion, or to use in their own writing, by having a word hunt as they read. You could group their choices into 'astonishing adjectives' or 'vibrant verbs' and display them.

- **Predicting**: Ask students questions that get them to predict what will happen next, thereby exhibiting their understanding of what they have read.

- **Quote quest**: Get students skimming and scanning a text to find quotations as supporting evidence.

- **Wall display**: You can chart an ongoing narrative, identifying key aspects of plot, character and interesting vocabulary, etc., by having an ongoing wall display added to each lesson as the reading progresses.

- **Story-mapping**: Like devising timelines or storyboards, creating a visual story map is a great way of tracking students' ongoing reading. They can include quotes, images and more.

- **Character profiles**: Get students to create ongoing reading records to track their developing understanding of characters, with appropriate evidence.

- **Triplicate note-making**: Students need to be trained in the art of note-making. Don't take it for granted. Rather than have them use a standard bullet point method for notes, get them to think a little more deeply. Divide the page into three. One, large column can include 'essential notes'. The second column can contain 'key questions', based on their reading. The final column is for 'mnemonics/images' related to their reading. This method not only gets students to record important information, it also gets them thinking more thoroughly about the text and it helps with embedding that information in their memory.

Post-reading strategies

- **Review writing**: Get students to consider the generic conventions of review writing.

- **Concept mapping**: These are structured maps (better than mind maps) that have a hierarchical structure facing downwards, representing relationships between characters/ideas, etc.

- **Student presentations**: Get students to present on an aspect of their reading, e.g. themes and ideas/characterisation/language and style.

- **Silent conversation**: Get students to note down their ideas based upon their reading, while paired partners '*respond*' to the point that has been made. The silence gets them focusing on representing their ideas clearly in writing.

- **Minor character method**: Get students to select a marginal character from the text and write their reflections on events/ summary of debates, etc.

- **Six degrees of separation**: Based on the theory propounded by **Frigyes Karinthy** (popularised by the Kevin Bacon game – 'six degrees of Kevin Bacon'), the goal is to connect characters/ ideas and themes, etc., from a given text in six steps. This gets students making sophisticated connections between and within the texts they are reading.

Pedagogy for teaching poetry

The study of poetry can be deeply contemplative or vibrantly active. It can often depend upon the poem chosen. Students can be sceptical about poetry. Perhaps endless close analysis can have a deadening effect, but poetry need not be taught in such a singular, monochromatic style. Here are some strategies to enliven and elucidate the study of poetry:

- **Sound the drums**: Borrow some real drums from your music department and bring rhythm and meter to life with some collaborative drumming. Bring iambs alive and use this strategy as a starting point to mark out poetry from prose.

- **Face the music**: Get students to bring in and research song lyrics. You can further illuminate different genres of poetry by aligning them with musical genres and lyrics.

- **Word sifting**: Use **www.wordsift.com** and paste the text of a poem, and it will organise the words alphabetically. This is a great way to break down just the vocabulary of a poem for close analysis. It can help reveal the tone and style of a poem in a unique fashion.

- **Poetry scramble**: To get students to focus on the form and structure of a poem, simply cut up or scramble the lines of the poem and get students to work in pairs or small groups to piece it back together, considering both the form and meaning.

- **Punctuating poetry**: An important aspect of much, but not all, poetry is how punctuation is used to adapt rhythms and to create meaning. Removing the punctuation and asking students to punctuate the poem themselves is a good way to lead them to analyse the effects created by different types of punctuation.

- **Performing poetry**: By getting students to perform poems in small groups, you can get them to consider closely what vocabulary choices require specific emphasis or choral effects. Different interpretations from different groups can spark illuminating debate.

- **Poetry paintings**: Many classic poems, such as Tennyson's 'The Lady of Shalott', have paintings based on the same theme and character. You can use these images, or create your own, as an effective pre-reading activity.

- **Poetry anthology writing**: Few other activities make poetry more comprehensible than the writing of poetry. Students write best when they are given parameters for their writing, such as specific genres and poetic techniques to use. Give students specific poetry writing tasks to guide them. For example, you could ask them to give a voice to an object in poetic form. Slyvia Plath's '**Mirror**' is a brilliant model.

- **Poetry templates**: You can use poems as a writing template, such as Kit Wright's fantastic poem, '**The Magic Box**'.

Pedagogy for teaching Shakespeare (and drama) in English

The teaching of Shakespeare is a compulsory component of every English curriculum. Great teaching of Shakespeare can be a feisty fusion of reading and drama. Students do struggle with the complexities of the language. It is a valid hurdle that we must overcome. Luckily, there are tried and tested teaching strategies that will help you teach Shakespeare more effectively:

- **Shakespearean insult kit**: A great way for students to get to grips with the Elizabethan language is to use this resource (easily found with an Internet search). Get them showering you with arcane insults and using the language of the Bard.

- **Shakespeare's inventive language**: Get students to research the words that Shakespeare invented. Get them to dig into the etymology of such words, building their expertise and confidence with the language.

- **Contextual research**: You can help bring Shakespeare's plays to life with some well-chosen contextual information. Debates about the marriage of young teens is one way to spark to life the arguments at the heart of *Romeo and Juliet,* or the misogynistic attitudes to women and *'witches'* that inform *Macbeth,* etc.

- **Creating a 'coat of arms'**: Get students to consider individual characters by devising an appropriate coat of arms.

- **Real-time researchers**: If you have access to tablet technology, or if you set specific homework researching aspects of an upcoming scene, you can help demystify the language and ideas of the play as you read it. Create research monitors whose job it is to seek out the etymology of certain word choices, etc.

- **Performing the play**: Shakespeare comes alive in action. There is no substitute for taking students to the theatre, but a best-case alternative is to have students perform the roles in the reading of the play. Students do benefit from seeing particular scenes performed (most plays have at least a couple of excellent versions) prior to reading the play, to bolster their understanding of the scene.

- **Modern translations**: There are many published and web-based translations of plays and specific scenes. These are a practical aid for students; however, we need to aim for balance, ensuring students engage with the original text with some detailed close reading.

- **Thought tracking**: Ask students what particular characters are thinking at given points in the play.

- **Conscience alley**: Students form an *'alleyway'* and direct questions relevant to the inner thoughts of a specific character. These questions can then be debated and answered.

- **Seven-word scenes**: Often best as a summative plenary, students summarise the story of a scene in only seven words. This reduction makes them make considered choices about the most important aspects of the play.

- **Soundscapes**: A good way to highlight the performative aspect of a play and to understand a scene is to create an appropriate soundscape that represents the mood and atmosphere related to characters, settings and scenes.

- **Freeze-framing**: An absolute drama staple. Select a crucial moment in the play to freeze. Discuss the significance of that dramatic pause, explore the positions of the characters and identify tension, etc. You could get students to select moments of extreme tension, melting the freeze-frame into other important momentary snapshots of the action.

- **Mime**: Cast out the image of the French mime artist sliding into your consciousness and consider the opportunities offered by muting the action and focusing in upon gesture, expression and movement. Done well, this drama technique will not only bathe your teaching group in serene silence, but it can also unveil hidden layers of meaning from any given text.

- **The guided tour**: Get students to grips with the relevance of the setting and staging of any play by undertaking a 'guided tour' of the set or the wider setting. Students could be in role as a director, introducing characters or their important props, unveiling the significance of the playwright's artistic choices.

- **Scene symbols**: Shakespeare is so rich with imagery that a good way to understand aspects of the plays is to explore symbols in detail. This could be creating symbol collages for plays or related to individual characters, or devising their own symbols to represent scenes, characters and settings.

Pedagogy to stimulate effective student talk

Language, and indeed the act of learning, is inherently a social act. When we read great literature, or write for an audience, we need to talk about, challenge and debate our ideas to build our knowledge and hone our skills. Of course, any effective classroom talk or group work requires training, with clear rules and high expectations.

Students need to be given explicit parameters and expectations for effective talk. Some basic expectations and standards of talk might include:

- **Active listening (see Chapter 7)**: Listening is paramount. Listening actively involves eye contact, positive body language and appropriate verbal responses. These need modelling and reinforcing on a consistent basis.

- **Standard English**: The *academic code* and language of your classroom will also require training. Aim to model and scaffold the use of standard English. Students benefit from being scaffolded to ensure their language is clear and specific: for example, recast the language of students so that they use *'protagonist'* rather than *'him'*, or encourage students to use discourse markers to organise their ideas and use sentence stems to formalise what they say, such as *'however, some may argue'* or *'furthermore, I believe . . .'*

- **Turn taking**: It may appear obvious, but establishing rules of polite turn-taking early on is essential.

Group talk can be one of the most effective methods to develop understanding. Students gain much more language input from their peers than they ever could from a teacher busy with a class full of students. That being said, such talk can flounder badly and perpetuate misunderstandings if it isn't structured carefully. Ensure that the parameters of their role, the timing of their talk and the exact nature of what their talk should remain focused upon are made explicit and clear.

Here are some effective group talk activities:

- **'Think–pair–share'**: An essential and simple approach. Let students think individually about a given question or topic, then allow paired discussion, before feedback is undertaken.

- **Snowballing**: Follow the steps of *'think–pair–share'* before, then *'snowball'* two pairings into a group of four for extended feedback – repeat ad infinitum!

- **Expert/home groupings**: For any given research activity, you could set up groups as *experts*. For example, if you were studying a literature text at KS5, you could ask one group to make notes on style and structure, another to focus on themes and ideas, etc. These *expert* groups then return to their usual *'home group'* and feed back their expert findings.

- **Debating**: Use clearly structured *'Oxford rules'* to engage students in a formal debate based on any given topic.

- **Socratic circles**: Students are arranged into inner and outer circles. The inner circle can discuss a topic or text, while the outer circle reflects upon the answers given. The outer circle members can be given specific roles, such as monitoring the quality of questions, focusing on the use of evidence in an argument, etc. The options really are endless.

- **Spotlighting**: With group discussion/debates/research, the teacher circles the room. They raise their arm by a specific group, thereby spotlighting that group, and the rest of the room becomes silent and listens in to the spotlighted group, whose members continue their talk. It is particularly effective for assessed speaking and listening. It is a good method to keep all students focused and on task, as they don't know when they will be asked to contribute.

Pedagogy to create a 'culture of enquiry'

Students, on average, ask only one question every six or seven hours in classrooms.[1] This may appear shockingly rare, but, when you consider you have large classrooms full of inquisitive students, it should not be wholly surprising.

We must, therefore, attempt to increase the volume and quality of questions in our classroom. Students deepen their understanding and knowledge when they ask *'why'* questions – those crucial questions that elaborate on what new knowledge they need to know and hook into their crucial prior knowledge. We need to create a *culture of enquiry* to make our students active and successful learners.

Here is a range of strategies to enrich the quality of questioning and to stimulate a positive culture of enquiry in your English lessons:

- **Key questions as learning objectives (LOs)**: What better way to foster a culture of enquiry than to spark the whole shooting match off with a big question that gets students thinking critically about what they are going to learn? By asking a big question, you can initiate thinking and group discussion that immediately engage students. The example 'How does John Steinbeck present the theme of friendship in contrast to the theme of loneliness?' can act as an LO, a great starter for discussion and even an effective plenary.

- **'If this is the answer ... what is the question?'**: Taken from the television show *Mock the Week*, this simple little technique sparks the innate inquisitiveness within students by quickly reversing the standard question and answer dichotomy. It could be a relatively closed answer, such as a character name, or something more open, such as a theme from a given text, such as 'religion'.

- **'Thunks'**: These little gems are great to initiate deeper thinking, with seemingly simple questions opening up a complex array of higher-order thinking. Thunks, such as 'Who would be the better prime minister? Sherlock Holmes or Dr Watson?', are great fun and thoughtful starters. These clever questions (see Ian Gilbert's excellent *Little Book of Thunks* or the website: **www.thunks.co.uk**) stimulate lots of interesting questions and debate. As the students become familiar with thunking, they can begin to formulate their own thunks.

- **'Just one more question ...'**: Given any topic or subject, students have to work collaboratively in groups to create an array of quality questions. They can then be given a series of challenging question stems to broaden their range of questions, using the following: *What if ...? Suppose we knew ...? What would change if ...?* If they write the questions on post-it notes, then they can be collated and saved. As the topic develops, students can add 'just one more question', as well as answering the initial questions as their understanding grows.

- **Question monitor**: This strategy constructively involves students in the evaluation of and reflection on the questioning process. A monitor, or a pair of monitors, would be given the responsibility to track and monitor the frequency of questions – teacher and student, open or closed, factual or conceptual. You can have them monitor for a given task, or relate more cumulative research by making it over a week or two of lessons. The activity sends a very powerful message to students about how highly you value quality questioning.

- **Question continuum**: The continuum involves the students first devising questions, in pairs or groups, on any given topic or idea. Then, the continuum is created very visibly, either on the whiteboard, or more semi-permanently on a display board (with student questions being on post-it notes for added flexibility). The horizontal axis could represent the 'interest level' generated by each question – that is, how likely the question is to inspire new thinking and new possibilities, or 'complexity' (from 'closed factual questions' to 'open, conceptual questions').

- **The Question Wall**: The 'Question Wall' is a working space for students to communicate questions about their learning.

Giving students post-it notes and asking them to commit questions to writing typically eliminate those questions that reflect 'learned helplessness' – the 'how do you spell such and such?', when they have a dictionary; or, 'what do we have to do?', in response to your lengthy and erudite explanation of the task at hand! To add a level of nuance to the wall, consider creating simple sections with simple labels; for example, closed questions are placed on the left-hand side of the wall; more open questions are placed progressively to the right.

Pedagogy for special starters

There is no formula for the perfect starter. Sometimes you need a settling, thoughtful strategy; at other times you want to spark them awake. Clearly, every teacher wants to hook the students into the learning of the lesson as soon as they enter the classroom. Of course, many English teachers begin their lessons with quiet reading, followed by a brief questioning session.

Cumulatively, all those starters add up to a considerable amount of reading, and, for many of our students, wider reading is essential to develop their vocabulary and so much more.

Here are some tried and tested starters for the English classroom:

Recapping prior learning

- **'Just a minute'**: A summary of their prior learning based on their topic. Give them parameters: no more than three fillers, no pauses, etc.

- **Short summaries**: Get students to summarise their prior learning on a given topic in ten words, then reduce to five words, before summarising with a single word . . . if they can.

- **Mapping prior learning**: Using graphical representations, such as concept maps or story maps, map out their prior learning. This is a particularly good retrieval task, which is really important to help students embed knowledge in their long-term memory.

- **Tension graphs**: Ideal for a novel or a play – represent the changing emotions throughout a given text. This works well with plays such as *Romeo and Juliet*, where you can chart the trajectories of love and hate throughout.

- **'Opinion continuum'**: Revisit questions on the topic and ask students for their opinion somewhere on the 'agree/disagree' or 'true/false' continuum. This can be done with students moving physically across the classroom, or by pinning post-it notes on a ready-made opinion line.

Sparking new ideas

- **Key questions**: Debating a key question related to the topic, e.g. 'What are the generic elements of a fairytale?', when studying the genre, is a good way to spark their prior knowledge and initiate ideas.

- **Thesaurus chorus**: The competitive seeking out of new synonyms to generate new vocabulary related to the topic. For original writing, this is an essential way to scaffold the complexity of their vocabulary choices.

- **Imaginative images**: Using images related to a topic of all types, from award-winning photography to student-made efforts, is great inspiration for ideas. These can be a starting point for debate, descriptive writing and much more.

- **Mystery object**: Select a mystery object related to the topic at hand. Then ask students to debate the meaning related to the object. This can spark interesting concepts you hadn't even considered. Alternatively, get students to bring their own object and relate it to a concept/idea/character, etc., and have other students debate the relative merits of the choice.

Pedagogy for powerful plenaries

Although there is no formula for the perfect lesson, ending with a plenary that ties together the strands of learning and evaluates the progress of the students is undoubtedly essential. Indeed, how could we plan where to go next, if we are not clear about what students have actually learned by the end of each lesson? For that very purpose, many teachers revisit the LO of the lesson. There are, of course, a myriad of ways to include powerful plenaries in English:

- **Plenary proverbs**: Have students individually, or in pairs, devise a proverb to summarise what they have learned in the lesson (often a recasting of the LO).

- **Confidence continuum**: Have students write their reflections upon their learning on a post-it note and place it on a continuum line from 'unconfident' to 'very confident'.

- **Exit post-it notes**: Have students write their feedback on the lesson on a post-it note, e.g. 'one thing that went well', posting it on the door on their way out.

- **'Three–two–one'**: When reviewing the lesson, ask students to identify *three* things that they have learned, two questions that they still have and *one* 'big idea' related to their learning.

- **'Where next?'**: Get students actively reflecting upon their learning by getting them to consider, discuss and feed back what they expect to learn next with a simple question.

- **'What we have learned is like …'**: Get students to consider conceptually how their learning connects with what they already know by using analogies, e.g. Poets using rhyme schemes and meter *is like* … [playing tennis with the net down, as Robert Frost famously said].

- **Graphic summary of the lesson**: Get students to create a step-by-step guide, a flowchart, story map or storyboard to represent what they have learned.

- **Newspaper headline**: It may appear simple, and it is, but getting students to summarise their learning in a tabloid and/or broadsheet headline style can result in real language experimentation and deep thinking about their learning.

- **Exemplar answers**: Few plenaries work better than a showcase, with constructive feedback, of models of students' work from the lesson. It can exemplify understanding, or diagnose misunderstanding, which is crucial for forward planning.

ACTIVITY

As coincidence may have it, you are teaching a new unit on a Shakespearean comedy – insert your preference here – to a group of Year 9s and a group of A level English literature students.

- Would you employ the same teaching and learning approaches with both groups?
- Would you need an equivalent 'culture of enquiry' in each group?
- Would the drama strategies be more useful for one group than the other?

TALKING POINTS

- This chapter contains a huge number of teaching strategies. It would not be advisable to try them all in any given week. With that in mind, what strategies would you prioritise for your teaching?
- How will you evaluate each strategy to judge its success? Can the strategy be improved, or should you trial an alternative approach?

- How will you best organise these strategies into a coherent sequence?

Note

1 Graesser, A. C., and Person, N. K. (1994) 'Question asking during tutoring', *American Educational Research Journal*, 31(1), 104–37.

3 Planning essentials

Lesson planning is one of those teaching activities that most obviously mark out the novice English teacher from the English teacher with a wealth of experience. You will likely hear many hoary tales of epic lesson plans: plans that meet a plethora of standards, cater for every human need imaginable and contain a wealth of activities worthy of a fun fair. Indeed, to the untrained eye, the nuances of good lesson planning may seem an impenetrable riddle.

Each lesson will take a disproportionately long time to plan in the early days. The happy truth is that, after much deliberate practice, the riddle becomes solvable. The template for a great lesson plan can quickly become intuitive, and the outcome of every lesson you teach will give you crucial feedback to improve – providing essential hints to help you improve your practice.

The concept of the 'aggregation of marginal gains', devised by British cycling chief Sir Dave Brailsford, actually provides a great analogy for producing a good lesson plan sequence. The idea is that teachers search out the many small improvements that students need to make in English, which, when aggregated, provide for a significant improvement. Ask yourself, what are the key learning gains you want your students to attain in this scheme of learning?

Planning essentials

What we need to do is to work out the end goal and then, in each lesson, identify what specific marginal gains students will undertake. Will they hone their use of punctuation for effect? Will they learn about gender in Elizabethan Britain? If students learn *something* every lesson, then over the course of the school year they will undoubtedly improve a great deal.

Ask yourself with each and every lesson plan: what are they really learning in this lesson?

When we speak of planning, we typically divide planning into the following time frames:

- **Short-term planning**: This defines planning on an individual lesson basis and anything up to a week or two of lesson planning. Individual teachers are typically responsible for such short-term lesson planning.

- **Medium-term planning**: This typically defines a scheme of work over a period of multiple weeks. Most commonly, such plans span a school half term and end with a definitive outcome and summative assessment. Many English departments collaborate on such medium-term planning to ensure common learning outcomes for all students.

- **Long-term planning**: This defines planning over the course of a year, or even over the course of a whole key stage. It is important to have a long-term plan, with a comprehensive coverage of crucial knowledge and skills that you want students to learn. Long-term planning is most typically led and coordinated by English subject leaders.

 You will undoubtedly receive lots of useful advice about lesson planning. You will be able to draw upon departmental resources (hopefully!) and, often, entire schemes of learning. There is also a wealth of online resources, from **www.tes.co.uk/teaching-resources** to very useful teacher blogs and specialist organisations such as the excellent **NATE**.

Some of the best advice about planning lessons is to be found in Ofsted's excellent **'Moving English forward'**.[1] That report has helpfully synthesised research on English lessons, from which we can glean the following principles:

Factors limiting learning in English lessons

- **Excessive pace:** In the bold pursuit of *'rapid progress'*, teachers attempted a plethora of activities at a lightning pace that simply didn't respond to the needs of the students.

- **Overloading of activities in a lesson:** Linked inextricably to *'excessive pace'*, there is a tendency, particularly when being observed, that leads teachers to attempt to showcase *every* teaching and learning strategy in their arsenal. The obvious problem is that students don't achieve any *deep learning* – there is little time left for reflection, consolidation or full, worthwhile feedback. Beware the false idol of *'rapid progress'*.

- **Inflexible planning:** It will be dealt with in the subsequent chapter, but a classic novice error is attempting to plough on with a plan, even when it clearly isn't working. Taking the temperature of a class and quickly diagnosing if they actually understand the topic are essential. Responding to such feedback is of paramount importance for effective learning.

- **Limited writing time:** Students were too often unable to actually practise their writing or explore their own ideas in any depth. A classic error for teachers at all stages is to focus too much on the *teaching* and not enough on the actual *learning*. Constant teacher talk does not allow students to build up their skill in independent writing (although little or no appropriate guiding teacher talk would be absurd). Aim for balance between imparting the knowledge and then allowing students to hone their skills relative to that knowledge.

Factors enhancing learning in English lessons

- **Teaching is clear**: Teachers need to be explicitly clear about the LOs, as the students need to know where they are going. Clarity is the key to effectiveness: clear explanations, clear instructions and clear objectives.

- **Teaching is flexible**: Plans are important, but you must be responsive to the needs of the students. They may completely misunderstand your adroitly crafted explanation. You need to respond and adapt accordingly. Many experienced teachers will inform you that one lesson plan taught to one Year 8 group, which works brilliantly, may just as easily flounder with a supposedly similar Year 8 grouping. Learning is never as linear, clear and predictable as we would hope. Have the courage to change your plan.

- **Tasks planned were meaningful**: Students need to understand the purpose of *why* they are learning. For example, you will likely meet with deep-rooted presumptions about Shakespeare that you may have to vigorously uproot! 'Why are we bothering with this old stuff Sir?' We must explain the connections between what we teach and what they learn. Also, where possible, we should create authentic tasks, real audiences and contexts in our lesson sequences that invest students with a purpose.

Know thy students

The scene is set: your first Year 9 class. First day. You are positively crackling with nervous energy. You have begun with poetry. Concise, emotional and clear. What could go wrong? You've hooked them in with breathtaking images and an artfully crafted explanation of the value of poetry. Now, the poem. Collective groans fill the room: 'Sir, we did this in Year 8!' Lessons are learned – quickly.

You need to know what they have been taught (knowing the primary curriculum is a great help), check previous schemes of learning, speak to teachers in the department and, of course, ask the students. Prior knowledge of the students and of their prior learning is essential.

Much is made of *personalising* planning for students. You need not fear twenty-eight separate lesson plans. Personalisation is when you attempt to synthesise your knowledge about your specific English group and you adapt your planning accordingly.

One of the ways you can quickly ascertain the 'how' and 'what' of your teaching is to get to grips with the student data. Luckily, most schools now gorge on data, like children with chocolate at Easter. For English teachers, having the right data and knowledge is crucial. Here are some starting points:

- **Reading ages**: These are done as part of the primary SATs, but many secondary schools also have students undertake a reading-age test. These data sets, although imperfect, are often excellent indicators of both reading skill and as a general barometer for progress in English.

- **SATs levels**: Like any external testing, students are, of course, primed to succeed, and, therefore, there can be distorted results; however, SATs levels are generally a reliable judgement.

- **School target grades/levels**: Almost all schools create their own internal target-setting system. Of course, schools are rightly aspirational about targets; therefore, don't be afraid to question their efficacy. That being said, once more, they are a good working target point, but don't slavishly adhere to such numerical values (English targets often miss the nuanced difference between reading, writing and speaking and listening levels and skills).

- **Special educational needs (SEN) information**: There is a legal requirement for us to know SEN information about physical, emotional and psychological needs. You're duty bound to know this information, but don't be frightened to seek advice. Your subject leader and/or special educational needs coordinator (SENCO) should advise you appropriately. Your planning should explicitly reflect any extraordinary learning needs, alongside more subtle personalisation for students.

- **The small details**: The little details often make the difference. Knowing the respective friendship groups, fallouts and changing relationships is often crucial when you are grouping students in a given lesson. Know this information – it is marginal but important. Data can be eminently useful, but our students aren't statistics. Each one is a living, breathing, complex mass of thoughts, feelings and no-little angst. Be kind. Get to know them as people.

Plan clear, effective lesson sequences

Lesson plans can often appear inscrutable to the untrained eye. To novices, connecting lessons in sequence can prove challenging, as they don't have the ingrained sense of timing common to the expert. With experience and deliberate practice comes the intuitive knowledge of such patterns (which brings with it the confidence to change plans when things aren't going as planned). A typical sequence of lessons may follow this pattern:

- **Activate prior knowledge**: Review their prior learning through teacher talk and questioning. Quiz, ask questions, initiate discussion. As noted already – you need to know what they know.

- **Teacher explanations of new knowledge**: Hook their interest; exemplify and make abstract concepts concrete. Clear step-by-step explanations are best accompanied by lots of questions to check understanding. This is the very essence of teaching!

- **Modelling and guided practice**: Students need to see what success looks like and they need to take their first steps with appropriate scaffolds and guidance. Show them great pieces of writing, or create one together.

- **Formative feedback on guided practice**: Students need to know how they are doing to get better and gain greater independence. This feedback may be given orally or in written form – and will involve the teacher and sometimes other students too, if appropriate.

- **Reflection on formative feedback**: Often a missed step, but a crucial one. Students need to reflect, then adapt and tweak their learning to improve. Lots of checking of understanding is required.

- **Independent practice**: We often speak of the value of independence in schools. This is an appropriate end goal, but that pathway is long and full of constructive guidance and meaningful repetition of skills. With writing, for example, students may independently write a poem, based on a lifetime of understanding of cultural and structural written references. They won't improve such writing with consistency if their practice is not laden with timely feedback.

- **More feedback and more reflection**: I'm sure you are detecting a pattern. The centrality of feedback and reflecting upon their learning, and the adjustments and improvements required, is at the very heart of great English teaching.

- **Repeat**: Any learning students undertake on any given topic in English is never really *finished*, particularly in a subject such as English, which has reading and writing skills that are always ripe for development, even far beyond what we understand as our conventional education. The cycle simply rotates, gathering knowledge with each turn.

This sequence is often repeated numerous times. No matter. Repetition should not be derided – it is pattern forming and habit forming. It allows students to transfer knowledge to their long-term memory, banked for future learning in English.

Planning essentials

Comfort and confidence arise from drilling specific skills. Embrace this fact and allow students to hone their skills in reading and writing until their skill becomes something like automatic – like riding a bike.

This sequence may occasionally occur in the span of one lesson, or over the course of ten lessons – based on the needs of the group and the complexity of the topic at hand.

Exemplar planning sequence: 'KS3 – Gothic writing: describing character'

• **Activate prior knowledge**	Have students work in pairs to *'think–pair–share'* and map their understanding of the term *'Gothic'* and related ideas. *'Snowball'* pairings into groups of four. Initiate whole-class feedback. Annotate an *'Uber-map'* that synthesises student feedback. Photograph the map to use in future and to recap knowledge
• **Teacher explanation of new knowledge**	The teacher leads an explanation that gives some of the milestones of the genre, from *The Castle of Otranto* to *Dracula.* The explanation focuses upon the key motifs used in the genre and its influence on contemporary culture. Targeted **probing questions** check student understanding
• **Modelling and guided practice**	Extracts from *Dracula* and *Frankenstein* are analysed, with teacher-led **text marking** and a close reading of stylistic devices to create a monstrous character. Students then continue a *Dracula* extract in the Gothic style

- **Formative feedback on guided practice**

  Students peer assess their writing practice (closely scaffolded), before reading their writing and receiving oral feedback from the teacher and from fellow students

- **Reflection on formative feedback**

  The students make targeted improvements to their writing, based upon their feedback. The teacher discusses the importance of drafting, and students share their adaptations and edits, with reasoning for their crafted improvements

- **Independent practice**

  The students are tasked with devising their own piece of Gothic descriptive writing: describing a monster akin to the Shelley and Bram Stoker extracts. They plan and draft their writing, using the '*uber-map*' as a memory aid. They then undertake a '**gallery critique**' to share precise peer feedback. Students draft improvements in light of this feedback

- **More feedback and more reflection**

  The teacher then assesses the final draft of their Gothic descriptive writing. Students are given formative feedback using the '**two stars and a wish**' model. Students respond to the feedback and outline their next steps for improvement

- **Repeat**

  The students have established the key elements of the Gothic genre. The teacher then focuses upon other aspects of Gothic writing, such as narrative perspective, the development of setting etc. A similar cycle of practice is undertaken.

Create a clear and coherent scheme of learning

Like any successful journey, the guide establishes the destination and then plots the route. The same is true of a good scheme of learning.

Take, for example, a KS4 scheme of learning based upon persuasive writing. The teacher would be wise to define a meaningful summative assessment to provide a worthwhile judgement of student progress in mastering the art of persuasive writing: creating a persuasive discourse structure, using rhetorical devices, writing with a clear sense of audience and clarity of argument, and writing with coherent accuracy of expression.

I have devised one such KS4 persuasive writing scheme of learning, with a summative assessment of students writing a formal letter to a local or national newspaper, writing persuasively about *teen role models* or the *dangers of reality television*. These outcomes were real and meaningful. They also displayed a close similarity to prospective KS4 examination writing outcomes.

The scheme effectively replicated the cycle outlined earlier in the chapter.

Humorous, engaging and persuasive articles (from, among others, journalists such as Charlie Brooker and Grace Dent) were analysed and critiqued as exemplar models. Students practised persuasive techniques in digestible chunks, repeating and adapting their use for effect. Feedback on their writing was crucial. The power of grammar was made explicit. Finally, students crafted and drafted their letters to fulfil their real-world purpose.

As identified in the Ofsted report, 'excessive detail' can have a detrimental impact. Define the knowledge and skills that you want students to develop and design an outcome that can aptly assess that knowledge. Break down the knowledge into understandable chunks, with lots of engaging models (including the work of the students themselves, as well as 'bad examples' that can be improved upon).

Yes, variety may well be the spice of life, but repetition and the 'deliberate practice' of a skill, over and over, until it is fully honed are also very important. Balance a variety of activities and engaging resources with rigorous repetition and you will have yourself a great scheme of learning.

Give it a go. Select a prospective scheme of learning. How will it match the cycle outlined in this chapter? How will repetition be used effectively? What knowledge and skills are essential?

ACTIVITY

Given the advice about planning a scheme of learning, and using the aforementioned Gothic writing model, devise an overarching plan for a scheme of learning.

- You have a six-week cycle of lessons. The topic is KS3 introduction to Romantic poetry. The end-of-scheme outcome is a comparative analysis of two famous Romantic poems.
- Your English department stock cupboard is bursting with William Wordsworth and William Blake, but there is an expectation that three poets are studied in some depth.

Map your planning sequence, using some of strategies introduced in Chapter 2.

Plan flexible lessons – identify and share progress

At the beginning of this chapter, I outlined the importance of 'flexibility'. As Robert Burns sagely noted: 'The best-laid schemes o' mice an' men / Gang aft agley'. Our best-laid lesson plans can fall deadly flat. Sometimes, irritatingly, an entire scheme of learning requires some major reconstruction in light of students not being able to access the new knowledge or a whole host of unpredictable reasons.

What is key is that, in every lesson, you explicitly plan for opportunities where students can share their progress, and you can tweak, or wholly transform, the teaching in direct response to student feedback. For example, if you undertake a question and answer session about the meaning of key words you have just explained, and students give faltering answers, then you likely need to explain once more, checking repeatedly to ascertain what they are not understanding.

Novice teachers often suffer the fate of such a failure of a lesson because they miss the small signs that students are missing the point – from minor, low-level disruption, to a usually switched-on student struggling to make sense of the task at hand. With experience comes your own intuitive Richter scale for learning.

To see the signs of successful progress, or imminent trouble, nice and early, it is important to embed checkpoints to exhibit progress (known as **formative assessment** – which is explained, with examples, in **Chapter 5**). This may be simply in the form of students' oral responses to questions, or reading aloud examples of their practice writing.

These are key 'hinge points' in your lesson, whereat you plan to adapt or continue your lesson plan (see **Using 'hinge point' strategies to identify formative progress,** in **Chapter 4**). The students may show they are dealing with the activity easily, and you therefore need to up the level of challenge; conversely, you may need to reiterate an explanation, or simplify a task, or omit a task altogether to allow you to consolidate their knowledge.

Often, simply stopping and reiterating the explanation does the trick. If, for example, students are struggling with essay writing, then, usually, modelling an exemplar paragraph will give them the clarity and impetus they need. Don't be worried about going *off piste* in terms of your plan – follow the learning and free yourself to deviate from the plan.

You may find you are being observed and are under pressure, or you have the pressure of completing a given piece of work for a specified deadline. Not adapting, changing or slowing down in any given lesson will have a more damaging impact on progress, in the short term and the long term.

A good tip in terms of long-term planning is to always allow for two or three fallow lessons, empty of planning, to allow you to catch up, make changes or compensate for the geography trip that you didn't know was happening!

Here are some of those telltale signs that students are struggling:

- **Low-level disruption**: Particularly from students who are typically focused and well behaved, but who obviously lack attention on the task at hand.

- **A critical mass of basic questions**: Sometimes, a litany of questions can be down to a learned helplessness from younger students, but sometimes a sequence of questions can set off warning lights that they simply don't understand – either what they need to do, or the content of what they are tackling.

- **A rising clamour**: Sometimes, a short way into the task, the students collectively begin to distract and disrupt. This can often correlate with a particular question or challenge that has stopped many students in their tracks.

Remember: Don't be afraid to ask students to 'stop, look and listen', before you *reiterate, rephrase* or *wholly recast* what they need to learn or *how* they need to learn. A lesson plan is not a stone tablet. It should be a flexible guide that you can adapt to meet the exact and changing needs of your students.

Using learning objectives effectively to guide learners

LOs are useful tools for setting a clear goal, with success criteria. Such LOs need to be challenging, set high standards, take into

Planning essentials

account the prior knowledge of students and have a clear and explicit use of language.

LOs are the signposts of learning. They come dressed in their own unique language that should be concise, specific and clear. Here is a simple and clear structure for creating LOs:

Sentence stem	Verb	Process	Purpose
I can	Select	Quotations from the novel	For successful essay writing
I can	Manipulate	Persuasive devices	To engage my audience

 Many teachers use **Bloom's taxonomy** or the **SOLO taxonomy** (if you haven't heard of these, get on the web and do some research – just don't get distracted!) to classify the complexity of LOs in their planning. It is worthwhile giving structure to your thinking by applying these taxonomies, but your students need not do so.

It is much more important that students are clear about the specific learning that they are undertaking (the action verb indicating the 'how') and the purpose of that learning (the 'why'). You may be absolutely clear about the LO, and that is what matters.

Many schools have a clear policy on LOs, but, if you have freedom to choose, then a flexible application of LOs is important. Having students write down LOs every lesson mechanistically can make students switch off to important information. The crucial factor is that teachers fully understand the LO of the lesson. Students may not need the signpost.

I have observed legions of great lessons that don't make LOs explicit as some easily digestible sentence, but where the teacher does clearly articulate goals for students.

Of course, many great English lessons veer from the *intended* goal, and often these rather unintentional lessons mine rich ground for learning!

Here are some strategies to vary your use of LOs:

- Use the same LO over more than one lesson and get students to recall the LO specifically.

- Recast the LO into a central question that students debate and feed back.

- Adapt the LO by employing a cloze exercise, omitting the key action verb (prior knowledge of typical verbs for LOs would typically be required here).

- Transfer the LO into a sequence of images that students need to translate (this typically takes some scaffolding and some practice!).

- Embed the LO into the opening explanation and get students to decide what the LO is, based upon the explanation. Once more, they will need a good working knowledge of LOs in order to complete this activity successfully.

- Hold the learning objective until the end of the lesson and discuss the purpose of the lesson, getting them to reflect more deeply on what they have learned.

Assessment as planning

Planning and assessment are inextricably linked. Any effective scheme of learning is built upon the skeleton of assessment, and, therefore, any planning sequence must take account of progress in lessons: either in the written mode or orally. Ongoing marking of students' work is one of the best ways to diagnose progress; therefore, we must specifically plan such diagnostic milestones of *formative assessment* (see **Chapter 4**).

Each English group, particularly in different key stages, may require different formative assessments. Here are some common strategies for creating assessment milestones, from which you can diagnose progress and adapt your future planning:

- **Comparison tasks**: A good way to assess formatively is to get students to complete tasks that can make comparisons between a whole host of concepts, ideas and texts. For example, you can judge the progress made with two recently taught poems by using a **Venn diagram** or a **'comparison alley' diagram** to analyse similarities and differences. By gathering oral feedback on such a task, or having students complete some written feedback, you can judge whether the poems need to be revisited, or if there are common misapprehensions or gaps in understanding related to the genre or topic more generally.

- **Evaluative discussion**: Get students discussing a concept or topic in an evaluative way and observe their interactions. The quality and depth of their responses, alongside a round of oral feedback, allow a good formative assessment, to judge whether the concept or knowledge has been fully understood.

- **'Three–two–one feedback'**: Get students to exhibit their understanding by completing this simple plenary task. On a given topic or lesson, students need to write three things they have learned from the topic/lesson, two questions that they still have and one 'big idea' related to their learning.

- **'Marking is in fact planning'**: By marking students' work, you are providing a highly personalised and differentiated starting point for learning. If you mark the work of your groups consistently, then you can make nuanced adaptations to your lesson planning and medium-term planning.

Reinforce knowledge and understanding

Becoming a great reader, writer or speaker is an endless marathon of practice. If students were the finished article just in time for their English GCSEs or A levels, we would be in a very clear-cut business. As you would expect, the skills and knowledge that attend English are far more nuanced. The learning process includes sudden illumination, forgetting, grinding improvements and years of repeated practice and **spaced repetition**: *the repetition of an idea or a concept repeatedly in the short term, and over the long term, to help lock knowledge in the long-term memory of our students.*

Our schemes of learning should integrate spaced repetition of key skills and knowledge. For example, in a reading scheme, you will likely plan for repeated opportunities for students to practise information retrieval.

A character profile may require the retrieval of supporting quotations. A *'story mapping'* exercise to identify key plot points may also require key supporting quotations. Therefore, the skill of information retrieval will be repeated and reinforced on a termly basis. Often, the students will need this fact foregrounded to link their learning.

Essential knowledge requires careful, planned repetition. Graham Nutthall,[2] in his book *The Hidden Lives of Learners*, identified the importance of spaced repetition. He identified that there should be short-term spacing between repeating new knowledge for students, with repeating an item of new knowledge three times a week being a decent guide. This could be repeating a fact at the beginning of a lesson and in the plenary at the end of the lesson, before revisiting the fact in a short starter in the subsequent lesson – common sense, really.

This evidence does impact upon our planning. We should evaluate exactly where we introduce, repeat and reinforce the key knowledge we wish to impart. Consider the following when planning for spaced repetition:

- starter tasks that explicitly revisit the core knowledge from students' prior learning;
- plenaries that revisit the core knowledge of their learning;
- LOs that repeat key subject-specific terms that you want students to know, use and remember;
- end-of-the-week review-style tasks, such as quizzes, 'mastery tests' or *Just a minute*-style tasks, to repeat and connect core knowledge;

Planning essentials

- schemes of learning and mid-term planning that identify which knowledge and skills require explicit repetition;
- working wall displays to record key words or display learning that encourages spaced repetition of core knowledge and key concepts. Just having the glossary related to a specific scheme of learning, such as a glossary of poetic terms when working on poetry analysis, is a simple but effective way to repeat the core knowledge you want students to commit to their long-term memory.

CASE STUDY: THE ART OF LESSON PLANNING

As a new teacher, lesson planning seemed to suck up almost all of my available time and energy. In particular, I wasted a lot of effort designing activities, rather than considering what my students needed to learn. In an increasingly obsessive quest for efficiency, the approach I've developed has five guiding principles:

1 **Time is precious**: Put more of it into long- and medium-term planning.

2 **Marking is planning**: Every time you mark students' work should be time spent working out what they need to do next.

3 **Focus on learning, not activities**: I am the enemy of activities! Loading lessons with things to do actively prevents students learning whatever your clear, thoughtful objective is.

4 **Know your students**: Good teaching is founded on good relationships. Use data and your knowledge of your students to write 'pen portraits' of five students in each of your classes every term. Communicate these with the students concerned and let them know that you are planning lessons 'just for them'.

5   **The one-in-four rule**: In any given week, I'll spend a disproportionate amount of time planning one or two lessons, but most will be put together in no more than five minutes. My formula tends to be that, if every fourth lesson for every class is a corker, all will be well.

I have utter contempt for planning pro formas; my lesson planning consists of considering the following questions:

- How will the last lesson relate to this lesson? All too often, the skills and knowledge learned in one lesson are not revisited the next (performing well doesn't always equate with deeper learning).
- Which students do I need to consider in this lesson? If you know your students well enough, you can use your 'pen portraits' to focus on a chosen student each lesson.
- What will the 'bell work' be? Lesson time is too precious to waste having students waiting for tardy classmates to arrive – give them something that they can get on with immediately, and don't be afraid to abandon it when you're ready to start the lesson proper.
- What are they learning, and what activities will they undertake in order to learn it? This is where most planning time gets wasted! Use shortcuts such as the **Learning Event Generator** (check Google) to ensure planning is focused on learning, not activities.
- How will we know what progress has been made? Don't worry about students' performance – how much closer are they to the goals set out in your medium-term plan? Tell 'em.

David Didau, Assistant Head Teacher and English Teacher (author of *The Perfect Ofsted English Lesson*)

> ## TALKING POINTS
>
> - What existing planning structures are there in your English department, e.g. existing schemes of learning or expectations about lesson structures?
> - What teaching sequences will be most appropriate, given the different topics you are required to teach and the range of students you are teaching in any given group?

Notes

1. This can be found on the Ofsted website here: www.ofsted.gov.uk/resources/moving-english-forward
2. Nutthall, G. (2007) *The Hidden Lives of Learners*, Wellington, New Zealand: New Zealand Council for Educational Research.

4 Assessment essentials

Assessment, and particularly testing, receives a lot of flak in the media. 'Exams are too easy', 'Standards are falling' and 'Wrong exam questions' regularly fill headline space. You would be forgiven for thinking you will be teaching in a test factory.

The English curriculum is subject to change, and models of assessment change with it, from exams and coursework, to the range of examination bodies and their own unique brand of assessment. The range can appear dizzying to any new teacher. It is important to unpick the complexities and to understand assessment in English.

It is crucial to delineate the different forms of assessment and their role in learning. The most crucial differentiation is between the two key modes of assessment:

1   **Formative assessment**: a range of informal, and some more formal, assessments undertaken during the learning process, used to identify student progress. It is assessment *for* learning. Formative assessment allows for crucial modifications in the subsequent teaching and learning approaches. Examples include oral feedback, quizzes, ongoing book marking, asking students to read their answers aloud, one-to-one discussion with students, etc.

2   **Summative assessment**: a typically formal assessment, or test, that makes a typically qualitative judgement of student progress over time. Unlike formative assessment, it is an assessment *of* learning. Examples: external examinations; mock examinations; coursework or controlled assessments; formal oral assessments.

Both types of assessment are important, but their functions are very different. Formative assessment serves to develop the learning of students, whereas summative assessment acts as the terminal judgement on student learning.

Both require our attention. In our daily pedagogy, formative assessment is rooted in almost every lesson we plan.

For each lesson that we plan, we must be aware of summative assessments students are developing towards. Yes, it is important to enjoy learning for its own sake; however, we must be pragmatic, as our students need to achieve the best English qualifications they can.

There is also very interesting research that challenges the notion that *only* formative assessment enhances learning. Students receive a 'testing effect'[1] from summative assessments, which describes the memorable effect of sitting a test. Put simply, sitting a more formal test, such as a mock examination, demands a difficult act of retrieving knowledge. This has been proven in studies to be more memorable than simply restudying information. This does not mean we should advocate endless testing, but testing with quality feedback should be embedded in our English lesson planning.

There is a veritable cottage industry of products that exists to service 'assessment for learning', or **AfL** – the commonly used acronym to describe formative assessment – from coloured cups, to lolly sticks and an array of cards, and other gimmicks. We must remember that, beyond the gimmickry, there is a proven wealth of evidence from highly respected educationalists. The likes of Dylan Wiliam, Paul Black and John Hattie have proven in their research that feedback, of the formative kind, is one of the chief factors in positively impacting upon student learning.

As identified in the previous chapter, we must plan student learning to embed opportunities for good-quality feedback in every English lesson. If we ask great questions and give students timely and purposeful feedback, we can help great learning happen. If we ensure that students gain a strong sense of what great English learning looks like and feels like, then we give students every opportunity to make assessment an important tool for learning.

Know your English specifications and assessments

English departments across Britain have students studying a range of different qualifications for different exam boards. For each and every qualification, it is essential that English teachers are wholly knowledgeable about what knowledge and skills are to be summatively assessed. It is also important, if we are to get students to internalise excellence in English, that they know what assessment foci they are ultimately working towards, for both internal and external assessments.

Most English departments will undertake moderation procedures that should thoroughly address summative assessments and ensure a consistency of teacher assessment. These moderation sessions are a great opportunity to learn. Experienced English teachers develop a near instinctive sense of such judgements, but a novice teacher needs to practise marking summative assessments with some regularity to become accurate.

Use every opportunity to get feedback on your marking, from English subject leaders and from online standardisation materials.

Here is some advice to English teachers looking to secure their summative assessment judgements:

- View and moderate as many examples of sample work that you can.

Assessment essentials

- Seek out examples of internal summative assessments – ask your fellow English teachers for work from previous students, particularly exemplar work saved as a model of good practice.

- Ask for feedback on samples of your assessed work. Your department should already do this in the form of departmental 'work scrutiny' approaches, but they may not be as frequent as you need in order to feel confident you are on the right track.

- Read recent exam reports.

- Ask to attend exam-board courses that provide the latest feedback on assessment, or source the materials from such training.

Every new teacher faces a vast mass of new information. Sometimes, it can feel like hunting the proverbial needle in a haystack. Make sure that you do source the exact information about the expected assessment for each and every qualification you teach.

Don't feel inhibited about asking your subject leader a myriad of questions to ensure that you are getting it right. The best teachers are humble and question everything in a positive way.

Read each course specification with care. Highlight the key information; for example: internal assessment word counts, exact assessment foci for exam questions, etc.

Also, aim to share this information with students, creating opportunities for peer and self-assessment. Often, in the course of your sharing information with students, they test your knowledge and the clarity of your thinking, in a good way.

Marking formatively in English

Ask an English teacher about the challenges of the role, and they will likely tell you that marking is *the* most significant challenge. It is simply the English teacher's beast of burden! Being forewarned is forearmed. Even though, at times, our marking load will be kryptonite to our proverbial super-teacher, we can better manage this burden.

Here are some tips to manage your marking:

- **Create a marking rota**: You will have a range of classes with a host of different assessments. You cannot always do this, but aim to plan ahead and stagger your marking to make it more manageable. A vast pile of unmarked books has a dispiriting effect on our willpower! Having a checklist to supplement your rota can often help inspire you, as you see yourself mastering the challenge. Disclaimer: sometimes you won't be able to follow your rota. Don't despair, but attempt to manage yourself to get back on track.

- **Create your own marking habits**: Like any habit forming, we need to develop typical cues to help condition ourselves to get through difficult challenges. For example, marking in the same place, at the same time daily, with some well-deserved rewards (for me, it is a bagful of sweets), can prove more effective for forming good habits.

- **Mark little and often (when you don't have to mark lots)**: You will have major assessment deadlines involving mock examinations or coursework, etc., but it pays to keep on top of your formative book marking in particular. Find a manageable routine and stick to it. Can you mark five books every evening before you leave school? Can you tackle six essays each evening for a week?

- **Follow your departmental marking policy**: Every school and every English department will have their own marking policy (or feedback policy). Know the policy intimately and stick to it. Students recognise when a teacher gives high-quality feedback and they will expect common patterns of comment-based feedback, targets, etc. Recognise the expected frequency of assessment. Once more, students have a keen sense of fairness and standards. Raise the bar in terms of feedback and you will invariably receive a good standard of student effort.

Assessment essentials

- **'Crack the code'**: Most English departments will share marking codes that structure feedback (such as the popular *'two stars and a wish'* method – identify two strengths in their work and one formative *wish* to improve) or identify errors of grammar, etc. Embed these codes deeply into your practice. They can often save you the time needed to write out full comments. See the case study below for further tips on using codes, and particularly the use of icons.

- **Plan peer and self-assessments to balance your marking**: Peer and self-assessments aren't inferior cop-outs, as long as students are well trained in the how and why of assessment. A balanced use of peer feedback, for example, can build a shared sense of assessment objectives. Used in moderation, peer and self-assessments aid great learning.

- **To grade or not to grade?** Research by Paul Black and Dylan Wiliam[2] proved that giving students a grade as part of their feedback actually erases the impact of the formative written feedback. Unless grades are essential, don't use them. Aim to make all your feedback developmental and formative, whenever possible (which is most of the time).

- **Set clear targets to improve**: Formative assessment is fundamentally about engineering continuous improvement to student learning. Set one or two clear and actionable targets for students to improve. Aim to be as specific as possible with your targets; for example, 'improve your vocabulary' would be much better as 'improve your vocabulary by using more complex adjectives and adverbs'. Give them time to discuss and get to grips with their target(s), otherwise all your work will have been for naught.

- **Targeted marking**: Aligned with the value of peer and self-assessment, marking absolutely everything a student produces can prove counter-productive. It can make students wholly dependent on feedback all the time. It may also leave you in a pit of exhaustion. Better to skillfully target what work you assess in English books, etc.

- **Ask for help**: Sometimes, your marking load will simply feel like it is too much. Do ask for help and don't suffer in isolation. Deadlines can be tweaked. Support and time for you can usually be found. Remember: we are not super-teachers with an in-human, endless reserve of energy. Marking effectively sometimes comes in peaks and troughs.

Here is a case study with a tried and tested tip for managing your marking:

CASE STUDY: MARKING ICONS SAVED ME TIME AND HELPED THEM IMPROVE

Marking books used to take me hours as I laboriously and painstakingly scribbled out individual comments for each pupil's work. With my six classes of 30 pupils, marking 180 books even once a week, taking roughly 5 minutes to read, check, correct and comment on each, took 15 hours – a part-time job just on marking – and seemed completely unworkable. But marking only every 2 weeks seemed equally unpalatable – if they had to wait eight lessons for any feedback from me, would they actually know how to improve?

Instead, I thought, what would maximum impact, minimum effort marking look like? I started using icons. It took me just one minute per book – meaning even if I marked every pupil's book every lesson, it would take me only 6 hours a week, or roughly an hour after school a day.

I wrote five questions as targets before I started marking, then scanned their answer, chose the best fit between the student's work and the five options, and drew an icon. At the start of the next lesson, I wrote the icons and questions on the board, and pupils wrote their question in their books. They got instant feedback and could take action to answer their question straight away.

> This made me realise that what matters most is how timely the feedback is. The instant feedback was so helpful for students because they had a new target to work on every single lesson. My starters were also sorted as they could action my targets if I devised them well. It meant I could sustain a tight cycle of marking without ever burning out. More than anything else I've done in English teaching, it has saved me hours while helping them improve.
>
> **Joe Kirby, Subject Leader of English**
> **(author of *How to Start on Teach First: English*)**

Using oral feedback as effective formative assessment in English

Assessment is too often assumed to be the summative judgement of students' work in the written mode. We take for granted that asking questions and eliciting quality answers verbally can be just as important as written feedback.

The best formative assessment is often undertaken right in the thick of a task – a quick discussion with a student, or a question-and-answer session for a portion of the lesson with an English group. We must privilege these instances of oral feedback in our lesson planning if students are to maximise their progression between summative assessments.

Here is a range of strategies to foreground oral feedback in English lessons:

- **Small-group discussion**: This simple strategy is highly effective in ensuring students scaffold one another's ideas, before whole-group feedback is undertaken. It gives students time to formulate an effective answer, while providing a useful sounding board for their ideas. Any effective discussion needs clear boundaries and a tangible outcome, otherwise they will chat about their favourite television show and worse. Sweat the details. *Do they have to make notes? Who is giving feedback and how?*

- **'Pose–pause–pounce–bounce'**: This is a real core strategy for great English teaching, or any teaching for that matter! The structure is simple. *Pose* a question, *pause* to give students wait time, *pounce* on a specifically targeted student, before finally *bouncing* the response to other students. The essential element is the *bounce*. This allows the teacher to snowball responses and get nuanced feedback, based on what the students know.

- **'ABC feedback'**: This strategy is the perfect partner for the aforementioned 'bounce' of student feedback. It stands for 'Agree with . . .', 'Build upon . . .' and 'Challenge . . .'. It is quick and easy shorthand to scaffold feedback *between* students. Much is made in education about 'outstanding' teaching strategies. Few strategies have the simplicity and power to elicit outstanding responses. Students have to listen attentively to one another, and understanding is layered with complexity when orchestrated deftly by the teacher.

- **Opinion lines**: Given a point of debate, e.g. 'How far is Lady Macbeth to blame for the downfall of her husband Macbeth?', students are asked to form an orderly line in the room (you can simply use crosses on a board or a display) that indicates where they are between 'Strongly agree' and 'Strongly disagree'. This creates a very obvious and memorable formative assessment opportunity. To take it further, students can debate their stance using ABC feedback.

- **One-to-one feedback:** Marking books or essays and giving written feedback a week or two later is often simply too late to provide meaningful formative feedback. Aim to plan opportunities in your English lessons to talk with students about their ongoing work and to check their English books, etc. With smaller classes, this often proves easier. If students can be writing away independently, this usually allows for some time for really purposeful formative assessment time. It allows you to take the temperature of how the class is going and gives you the feedback you need for your subsequent planning.

Using 'hinge point' strategies to identify formative progress

One of the classic own goals an English teacher can score is to plough on with a planned scheme of learning, regardless of how the students are faring. We are often caught up in a mad rush for curriculum content coverage, at the expense of the quality of learning.

We need to have 'hinge points' in each lesson where we evaluate precisely in which direction the lesson needs to move. We need not fear if we have to return to where we started and reiterate instructions or effectively repeat the learning.

Hinge-point *questions*, as the name implies, are based upon a central concept in the lesson that needs to be understood for students to move forward. It is often a simple multiple-choice question, whereat every student gets a chance to exemplify their understanding, rather than one or two students ferociously spearing their arm into the air to dominate all the questions from the teacher!

Hinge-point questions have the added benefit of making misconceptions visible. Often, error finding can be just as productive as a learning experience as 'getting it right'.

Here are a couple of examples of English hinge-point questions:

- What is the correct definition of the rhetorical device *anaphora*?

  (a) The repetition of an 's' consonant sound.

  (b) Repeating words at the end of clauses.

  (c) Repeating words at the beginning of clauses.

  (d) The repetition of a vowel sound.

This hinge-point question can be particularly useful in diagnosing an important element of knowledge (the answer being (c)), while also providing a natural step towards its sister rhetorical device – *epistrophe* (defined by (b)). Another hinge-point question type can involve using four pieces of writing from the first part of the lesson and asking students to identify an element of knowledge you have expected students to learn. For example:

- Which text uses a combination of hyperbole, repetition and statistics to persuade its target audience?
  - (a) Text a: holiday resort leaflet.
  - (b) Text b: chocolate advert.
  - (c) Text c: political speech.
  - (d) Text d: newspaper editorial.

The concept of hinge points also extends to wider strategies – representing any formative assessment that is a potentially crucial turning point in any planned sequence of English lessons. Hinge points exist at the ends of lessons. Plenaries such as **Exit post-it notes** (see **Chapter 2**) can provide a hinge point at the end of a lesson, or a strategy such as **Twenty questions** can provide a formative hinge point at the very start of a lesson, or even the beginning of a scheme of learning:

- **Exit tickets**: This can be an opportunity for students to write down observations about what they have learned, ask questions that are still lingering related to the topic at hand, answer a summative question based on the lesson content. The 'tickets' can be simple post-it notes or small pieces of paper. Good exit tickets can actually provide a great starting point in subsequent lessons to recap upon prior learning.

- **Twenty questions**: It is simply an opportunity for students to generate a host of questions related to any topic (it works particularly well at the beginning of a new topic). The quality and scope of such a collection of questions can be really illuminative and pinpoint the prior knowledge of students, so that you can teach to their ZPD with real precision.

You can also create hinge points in schemes of learning by having 'mini-tasks'. A mini-task is, in effect, a microcosm of any end outcome. If students were working towards an analytical essay based on a class novel, then a mini-task would be an exemplar paragraph. By giving formative feedback on what is effectively a microcosm of the ultimate outcome, you can give students very purposeful feedback.

Purposeful peer and self-assessment

Some people deride peer and self-assessment as a short cut to teacher assessment. Truthfully, in my experience, students do express a preference for teacher-led assessment, but this reliance upon the teacher isn't always what is best for students. It may hint at the fact that, in many instances, peer and self-assessment is not done well.

Helping students internalise and use assessment criteria can be an important *metacognitive* strategy – that is, helping students better understand the assessment process – allowing them to recognise their own mistakes and subsequently correct them.

With the right tools and training, peer and self-assessment can be highly effective. It can help you manage your assessment load, but, if the pedagogy is soundly rooted in AfL, it can help students illuminate the success criteria of a given English task in an active and powerful way.

There are undoubtedly clear parameters and principles for successful peer and self-assessment. These involve some or all of the following:

- Take the time to fully *train* students to peer and self-assess, giving them explicit parameters, such as their comments needing to be constructive and precise (not just '*Great work!x*').

- Model the quality of assessment you want. Showing students model summative comments and marginal comments on writing simply scaffolds better feedback.

- Consistently share success criteria and decode the language of assessment for students. Do be wary of diluting the language of assessment foci to 'student speak' to the point of being simple and rather meaningless.

- Be systematic with using codes. With literacy codes, or common marginal comments, you need to use them consistently with students, so that they can build confidence and understanding in using them well.

- Follow any whole-school marking policies. Once more, it is about being consistent. Students clearly develop their understanding through repetition. If there is a common method and/or protocols for peer and self-assessment across the school, then employ them in English. If there is an expectation for whole-school proofreading strategies to improve literacy, then exploit the prior knowledge of the students.

- Allow time for students to write purposeful comments. Ensure students expect you to seek verbal feedback on their feedback. After some peer or self-assessment, question individual students about the comments they made. When they know this happens consistently, they will focus better on the task.

- Assess their assessment. It is important that you devote time to reflecting upon and sharing examples of student feedback. To ensure accuracy, you can actually ask students to self-assess their own writing (ideally, with well-modelled success criteria) before you then assess their writing. This saves time, while helping you scaffold high-quality self-assessment.

- As part of the process of self-assessment, get students to self-report their grades (identified by John Hattie[3] as a tremendously high-impact teaching strategy). For an exam, get students to self-report their expected grade. This process can be inspiring, as, when students achieve beyond their expectations, the confidence they gain can be truly transformative.

Helpful revision strategies for summative assessments

There is a wealth of research that supports the effectiveness of specific revision strategies over others. It is important to differentiate between being busy and undertaking productive revision. For example, simply rereading exam texts or notes has a low impact in terms of long-term memory retention. Compare them with other knowledge-retrieval tasks, such as making 'concept maps' in groups, which is supported by cognitive science research proving it to be more effective.

As you would expect, repetition helps students remember. We can be more specific about how we should structure our revision by again seeking out useful research.

We should ask ourselves how we structure our planning, both in terms of individual lessons and whole-year plans, to maximise the ability of students to remember what they have learned in English. By splitting up topics and returning to them intermittently, a couple of weeks or even months later, we can actually help improve the memory retention of our students.

Here are other strategies that support student revision for English summative assessments:

- **Concept map**: This is an ideal tool for helping people retrieve what they know and realise what they don't know. Think of *concept mapping* as the big brother of mind-mapping, without the annoying branding issues! The map is structured like a hierarchical flowchart. For example, if students are exploring the themes of power in *Dracula*, they make a hierarchical map of characters, with linked scenes and quotations, etc. Once they have tried to remember what they can without their notes, they can then fill in the gaps. This can be done collaboratively or individually. It can be done at the end of each week to recap the prior learning, etc.

- **Using worked examples**: Students can collaborate in pairs or groups to work on writing model exam answers or comparing such answers. They can rewrite a flawed model answer, grade good examples – the list is endless. You can take this one step further by having them present their model to the group, explaining their choices. This *reciprocal teaching* can ensure that students are actively engaging with the key choices in terms of the writing process they will need to make under the pressure and stress of exam conditions.

- **Regular tests or quizzes**. The very act of struggling to remember and retrieve information helps you remember what you have learned better. Therefore, having this process regularly planned into our English lessons can better diagnose areas where students are struggling and, hopefully, remedy the issue. The *'testing effect'* works, but overdoing it would deaden the learning experience for students and, perhaps, have the opposite effect to what we actually intended.

- **Collaborative retrieval tasks**: By having students work together to remember what they know, either in concept map-making, presentations on learned material or simply discussion, note-making and feedback, you can get students making a whole host of effective cues to remembering what they need to know.

- Other strategies already explained in the book, such as **shared writing** and *Just a minute*, would work equally well to fulfil the criteria of the strategies above. They all provide good assessment opportunities, which alert both the English teacher and the students about where they need to go next with their learning.

ACTIVITIES

After reading a chapter on planning and assessment, you are now an old hand and you are ready to combine the two.

First, you could take the Shakespeare task at the end of the last chapter. Look at your planning overview and consider:

- Where would you include formative and summative assessment points?
- What information would you need to repeat?
- Would your assessment methods be radically different for KS3 and KS5 students?

A second task would be to devise a new scheme of work for a mixed KS4 group. They are studying a Victorian novel (take your choice), and their summative assessment is an essay based on the central character of the novel. You have a half term of study: roughly six weeks.

Consider the following:

- What formative assessments will best establish their prior knowledge about the novel and their essay-writing skills?
- What would be your step-by step-learning objectives? What is the key knowledge you need to convey in this unit of work?
- What student work from the unit would you need to mark to best judge the quality of the learning?

TALKING POINTS

- What courses and specifications are currently to be undertaken in your school? Where are the best sources of information for these courses?
- What formative assessment methods will be at the heart of your teaching repertoire?
- How will you best manage your assessment workload? What habits do you need to establish?

Notes

1   Roediger, H. L., and Karpicke, J. (2006) 'Test-enhanced learning: taking memory tests improves long-term retention', *Psychological Science Journal*, 17(3), 249–55.

2   Black, P., and Wiliam, D. (1990) *Inside the Black Box*, London: GL Assessment.

3   Hattie, J. (2011) *Visible Learning for Teachers*, London: Routledge.

5 Differentiation in English

It is of crucial importance to define what differentiation is and what it is not. There are some exaggerated claims that differentiation in English is a vast array of personalised activities, with bespoke resources, all sliced and diced for individual students. It is not. Differentiation is happening in every lesson, in almost every moment, as teachers question and support students, adapting their lesson appropriately.

Despite popular misconception, every class is a mixed-ability class, and every student has talents and needs.

Most schools have their own model of class groupings that impacts differentiation: from **streaming** (grouping students by ability across subjects), to **setting** (grouping by ability in individual subjects) and **mixed ability** (classes that include a broad ability range). Each model has caveats and nuanced differences. These models can significantly alter the dynamic of the teaching and learning.

With a notional 'top set' (high-ability) English GCSE KS4 class, a teacher may well set more challenging tasks and expect a faster rate of progress. That is not to say that standards for all groups and all students should not be sky high – regardless of their current grouping. Consider the power of the '**Pygmalion effect**': that the greater our expectations of students, the better their ultimate performance.

Differentiation is commonly depicted as a focus upon students with SEN. Indeed, many students who do have specific needs, such as dyslexic and partially sighted students, may well need structured activities and resources that are overtly differentiated.

Too often, however, it is forgotten that differentiation also applies to challenging the most able, or responding to the host of subtle social and emotional needs you will identify. Students develop in stages, not ages. Many summative assessments simply don't capture the nuances of this development. In essence, differentiation is about knowing your students in all of their glorious complexity.

Every student needs to be appropriately challenged. This may manifest itself in the form of a challenging, open-ended question, or by having a choice of task or a meaningful extension task. The very notion of 'challenge' is subtle and complex. Therefore, it requires a highly attuned knowledge of our English students and their relative knowledge and skills.

The following are some key messages about differentiation:

- It is not twenty-six different lesson plans, or multi-styled resources.

- It doesn't have to be solely differentiation by resource or task. For example, differentiated questioning can be a powerful source of challenge for all.

- It is imperative we really know the students in front of us.

- Every student requires differentiation of a sort, but it can be subtle and requires consideration and careful planning.

Know thy students . . . even better!

As indicated in the planning chapter, knowing what the students know is a key starting point for all planning and teaching. That knowledge is broad in scope. Starting simply, knowing the students' names is paramount. In a short time, you will have a composite knowledge of the skills and knowledge of each individual student, combining prior attainment in external and internal assessment with more nuanced judgements about their capacity socially and emotionally.

For example, it is important to know which words individual students struggle to decode, but it is just as important knowing their confidence levels when asked to read in front of the class, or how well they work within a group-discussion task.

The question we should always have on our lips is 'how well do we know our students?'.

As noted earlier, some data and knowledge about students are valuable; some are not. You do want to keep an effective record of progress to support your teaching. Select good data, record them and use them. You can then identify early on the students who need the most support and act accordingly. Here is where formative assessment once again proves essential. It is the brief questions, the five minutes taken to mark a quiz or to scan their English book that give us valuable information.

Whether it is young Claire who needs support with spelling strategies, or little Jim who is mortified by the thought of reading aloud in class, knowledge of your students is indeed power. Sometimes, you need to look behind the data numbers and recognise the underlying issues, or indeed strengths, that make for students learning in different ways and at different rates.

Here are some data milestones to help you better know your students, with some attendant advice:

- **KS2 SATs tests**: Like any high-stakes external examination, students are primed and prepared to succeed in SATs. Results may, therefore, be skewed from hothousing for an exam, or from a uniquely poor performance on any given day. That being said, they typically give a sound baseline for making judgements on the reading and writing ability of our students. The SATs are currently levelled using numerical levels – level 4 being a typical national average that is reached by most students in England.

- **School targets**: Most school targets are aspirational targets, based on prior results from the SATs examinations and more at KS3. They are typically a very useful measure against which to judge their KS3 summative assessments. AT GCSE, many schools use **Fischer Family Trust** grade estimates or **RAISE Online** data. Of course, these targets aren't always right, and they are not set in stone, so do not fear to challenge them if you think they appear inaccurate based on your teacher assessments, both formative and summative.

- **Reading ages**: There are a few different pre-packaged reading tests that can generate a reading age based upon a short test of comprehension skills and vocabulary recognition. These results are typically accurate and very useful for deciding upon appropriate reading materials for individual students and for choosing a class novel.

- **SEN information**: Schools are required to record and disseminate a range of information about SEN. Your SENCO will be the crucial conduit for such information, so pursue their expertise. For example, they will be able to support you with specific information and resources regarding dyslexia if you have specific students with that SEN.

- **Pastoral information**: Good schools not only effectively share 'hard data', but they also communicate a host of personal and pastoral information about students. It can be an issue to do with attendance, or sharing knowledge regarding bullying or friendship issues that it is imperative for teachers to be aware of when planning to differentiate groupings for instance. If you are looking to better support a challenging student, for example, you should be able to garner useful information from their form tutor or head of year/head of house.

Challenge

Differentiation can wrongly become a synonym for dumbing down or a simplification of learning in the English classroom. Instead, we should view it as wholly synonymous with the concept of challenge.

Differentiation should actually represent a process of careful planning that enshrines the highest of expectations for students across the spectrum of ability.

There are a host of ways that you can ensure every student is appropriately challenged. When you know the prior knowledge of your students, you can better select appropriate reading material, or define writing tasks that allow for students themselves to maximise their potential. If we are to differentiate effectively, we need to know what they already know.

Here are some useful tips to ensure your students are appropriately challenged:

- **Have a range of teaching strategies**. Some students who struggle with writing benefit greatly from debating a topic and engaging in oral rehearsal. The opposite can also be true. Other students, lacking confidence in their speaking skills, are aided by scripting their ideas. Therefore, teaching and learning strategies need to be varied to suit the needs of all learners. By doing this, we can give students the confidence to master challenges.

- **Choice**: Choice can have a powerful emotional impact upon students. It can help scaffold their understanding, while building their confidence, allowing them to select which approach is most appropriate to them. A good example would be to get students to choose the success criteria for a given task. This simple strategy has added benefit in terms of *meta-cognition* – helping students recognise *how* they learn. Allowing a choice of task can greatly enhance their level of intrinsic motivation.

- **Get them reading**. Most students who underachieve in English are struggling readers who read below their chronological age. Many no longer enjoy the challenge of reading – it is too fraught with difficulty. Our challenge is to get them reading. Spend time sourcing the best reading resources – reading lists from librarians or students themselves – and create regular slots for reading in your weekly plans. Support parents in supporting their child to read. In lessons, talk about reading for pleasure; select a rich diversity of the classics and the contemporary and doggedly promote reading.

- **Find real audiences**. Students always rise to the challenge of writing or performing for a real audience. Provide an authentic audience for their writing – either their peers (using tools such as **Google Docs**), their local community (organising presentations or performances in the local area, e.g. a presentation being displayed in the local library) or the world (blogging or videos on **YouTube**, etc.)

Using support resources

Differentiation shouldn't ever be about felling a forest to provide a host of differentiated worksheets. Well-targeted support resources can prove to be a crucial tool that enables your students to succeed.

Here are some typical support resources to utilise in the English classroom:

- **Dictionary/thesaurus**: There is a wealth of school-specific dictionary/thesaurus options, from phonic dictionaries and concise dictionaries to weighty tomes. Have a range for every occasion.

- **Word banks**: These perform a similar role to dictionaries, but with the added benefit of chunking more subject-specific language into specific groupings. You can create your own for grammar word groups, descriptive writing and persuasive writing, or by genre.

- **Writing mats**:[1] Many schools have created their own literacy mats (freely available on the web) tailored to their students. They typically include high-frequency misspellings, homonyms, discourse markers, spelling rules, punctuation definitions, etc. Go one step further and create your own writing mats with students, using a blank template.

- **Working wall displays**: These can combine word banks, writing mats, etc., with constant development and adaptation. For example, you can add new, subject-specific terms as the scheme of learning develops. A word of caution: avoid creating little more than distracting wallpaper. This is not a good use of your precious time!

- **Writing frames**: Sometimes, it is appropriate to scaffold early attempts at writing. For a first-ever extended essay, for example, a paragraph plan structure can be an essential scaffold. Alternatively, a sentence starter can have a powerful impact, getting students over the common cognitive hump of simply making a start.

- **Exemplar models**: I have already stressed the timeless value of modelling. Using writing models can make the process of writing more accessible and give students a template for what success looks and feels like. Even a bad model can be instructive, often providing a fun way into writing practice.

- **Worked examples**: A teacher leading the modelling of writing, such as with an exemplar paragraph of an essay, can unveil the mysteries of *expert* writing, while also showing students that all writers make mistakes, edits, etc. Aim to explain the decisions you are undertaking as you make them, such as word choices or edits, while questioning students about those choices.

- **Student-led creation of support resources**: One way to differentiate for the most able is to have them lead the creation of support resources. They can thereby reflect upon and deepen their knowledge of the relevant success criteria for a given task.

Of course, you could make the student the resource, creating 'peer experts'.

Differentiation by instruction and questioning

A great English teacher develops the legion of marginal improvements to their teaching in a way that can be almost imperceptible to the novice. Don't fear! Some more obvious patterns emerge to reveal the subtleties of differentiated instruction.

Students of all abilities rely dependently upon their English teacher for new knowledge. Typically, effective instruction then proceeds through *interdependence*, whereat students are given worked examples and models to work from, or the teacher leads shared writing. Finally, independent study is the zenith of differentiated instruction. Aim for this process of gradual instruction, marginally raising the degree of challenge and providing apt support along the way. Such gradual, differentiated instruction is outlined here:

- **Differentiated instructions**: Give multiple examples to prove the core message of your explanation. For example, if you are exploring family conflict in *Romeo and Juliet*, you may want to give multiple analogies of similar conflicts, such as the accessible analogy of rival football clubs. It is about activating their prior knowledge, first and foremost.

- **Students reiterate instructions**: A good way to judge whether students have understood a complex explanation is by simply asking specific students to reiterate the information. The condensed repetition helps students and you in knowing whether representative students grasp the learning.

- **Differentiated questioning**: There are many methods to allow for differentiated questions. Providing multiple-choice answers, of course, aids students in making educated guesses. Having multiple 'right' answers can challenge the most able students.

By knowing each individual student, you can target your questions in their ZPD. Some students may require less challenging *closed* questions, such as 'Who is Mercutio's best friend in *Romeo and Juliet?*', followed by more challenging open questions, such as 'Why does Mercutio and Romeo's friendship result in conflict?'.

- **Repeat and check student understanding**: A simple and useful mnemonic to use with students is **KWL**: 'What do I **know**?', 'What do I **want** to know?' and, 'What did I **learn**?'. The underlying principle is to ensure students understand the LO, reflecting upon their learning (again, the concept of meta-cognition proves to be important for differentiation).

- **Question time**: Allow specific slots for students to ask questions of the teacher, and one another. For example, ten minutes into a challenging writing task (before that point, expect the highest standard of focused and independent writing) offer *Question time*. This typically has the added benefit of eliminating 'learned helplessness' questions in the first five minutes of any given task.

Differentiation by grouping

One of the most important tools of differentiation for students is . . . well, other students. As I have stated, *every group is a mixed ability group that requires differentiation*. If you 'know thy student', you can adroitly group students to support one another by balancing strengths and weaknesses and varying the grouping dynamic by personalities and/or by gender.

Many classrooms' seating arrangements account for such nuanced selections. Some teachers prefer grouped table designs, whereas others prefer individual or paired tables. There is no definitive evidence for the efficacy of one seating arrangement over another.

Check out what approaches colleagues in your department take. Ask yourself: will they work for your group? Ultimately, a crucial aspect of pedagogy is being flexible and changing and adapting groupings to ensure everyone has a high degree of challenge in their learning.

In English, peer communication is undoubtedly at the root of developing successful learners. Graham Nuttall's research in *The Hidden Lives of Learners* stated that, whether we like it or not, students receive most of their feedback from other students, often unsolicited. We must, therefore, group with the utmost care, continuously reflecting upon its effectiveness. Here are some common options for grouping:

- **Grouping by similar ability**: Grouping students in this way can allow for targeted teacher support. High achieving students can challenge one another, while typically working at a similar rate in terms of time. When using models, you can target their ZPD with accuracy. For example, with a peer assessment activity, you can have a group of students currently working at C grade level unpick and assess some B grade essays, so that they can understand their crucial next steps.

- **Grouping by mixed ability**: Selecting students to work in groups with different strengths and weaknesses can ensure that those students confident in their skills can support other learners. Not only that, they deepen their own understanding in the process of mediating between their peers. This is not the teacher resolving to ignore their own responsibility, but a recognition of the complexity of learning and the sometimes-foolish concept that students have a fixed level of ability that does not fluctuate from task to task.

- **Grouping by gender or 'personality'**: Relationships matter. Classrooms are a teeming mass of fluctuating relationships. *EastEnders* can have nothing on your Year 9 English classes at times! You need to be pragmatic and find a balance throughout the classroom. Be flexible and responsive.

- **Multiple groupings**: Some teachers and English departments run multiple groupings. For example, you can have three groupings, labelled as a variety of colours, one by friendship groups, another by ability and another by gender. The variations are endless. Early on, the practical stability of one grouping may well be best advised, but, as you develop your practice, your groupings may become more nuanced and involve changes to seating plans for given activities. For example, for a debate activity, a horseshoe-shaped seating style may work well; for a group discussion, then group tables would be advised, and so on.

- **Keep it fresh**: Consider changing your seating plans wholesale on a half-termly basis. Students need the richness and variety of working with someone new as much as we do. Again, be pragmatic if you have found a magical balance. It is a rare thing – keep it!

- **Be flexible**: Too often, we can settle into the habits of having students work with the same people, sometimes reinforcing the same misinformation, etc. We should not be beholden to a seating plan. Using strategies such as *snowballing* and *jigsaw* grouping (as described in **Chapter 2**) can ensure we vary peer communication.

- **Get competitive**: Students often enjoy working in teams. There is the danger of students taking a back seat during group work, but, like any good pedagogy, students need to be well trained. You can differentiate further by allocating specific roles. By establishing clear parameters for role, timing and outcome, you can harness the collective knowledge and skills of students who are very different in terms of need and talent.

Differentiation by outcome

As outlined in my planning chapter (**Chapter 3**), an effective sequence of learning will typically move from more guided and structured learning towards more independent and often open-ended outcomes. Simply, you can have tasks of differing degrees of complexity and length. A well-defined outcome allows all learners to access it successfully, while providing a strong degree of challenge for students of every need and talent.

Here are some methods to refine outcomes to allow for more personalised differentiation:

- **Providing learning scaffolds**: Providing *optional* learning scaffolds is an effective method of differentiating the outcome. Asking for a common outcome, such as a persuasive argument for a magazine editorial, can be refined with a simple instruction that they *could* use a five-paragraph structure, including a counter-argument (something like this: (1) introduction, (2) personal anecdotes, (3) factual evidence and opinions, (4) counter-argument, (5) conclusion). This can have limiting effects of course, but, by making it optional, you are subtly differentiating the outcome for all.

- **Provide the content and focus on the structure**: It is often the case that students need to grasp the conventions of a written genre. To allow students to concentrate on structural features of writing, you can provide them with the indicative content (the answers), thereby allowing them to focus wholly on crafting the structure of their writing.

- **Choice of outcomes**: Often, by offering a choice of outcome, you can allow students to define their own proximal development (although this is sometimes neither advisable nor practical). This can heighten their emotional investment in the task, while creating a rich variety of outcomes, which, when shared, can enrich the understanding of all students.

- **Open-ended outcomes**: By creating outcomes with elements of both choice and personalisation, you can naturally differentiate. For example, a speaking and listening presentation on Shakespeare's Sonnets can allow students to select their own resources, and they are free, with a degree of creative licence that can stretch their capacity to learn. It does help if there are agreed parameters outlined for the success criteria for such a task.

- **Outcome differentiated by length**: Too often we associate quality with quantity. Some students internalise this mistake, producing epic pieces of writing that are as shapeless as fog! Asking students to compress their writing down to a specific word count forces them to be more selective with their writing choices, often drafting with greater care and attention. Weaker writers are not overburdened by a monstrous word count, and yet expert writers are forced to hone and craft their writing.

- **Mini-tasks**: By asking students to write mini-versions of the extended outcome, you can provide useful formative feedback about their learning that can then effectively differentiate their ultimate outcome.

Differentiation using teaching assistants

There are few more valuable sources of support for an English teacher than their teaching assistants. They can provide the proverbial life-saving support when you are mired in the mud of a difficult lesson. Seize upon their expertise and their intimate SEN knowledge of each student.

Speak to them, often – before the lesson ideally – about planning and involve them in the process. Learn what they are most comfortable undertaking in terms of contributing and exploit their excellence.

Some new teachers fear having another adult in the room, particularly when things are going badly wrong. Remember: teaching assistants are not sitting in judgement of your teaching – they are willing you to succeed. Students are acutely sensitive to hierarchies. Like wolves, they can sense status in the pack. Ensure you promote the status of your TA appropriately, involve them and let them take a lead. Here is some guidance for working with your teaching assistant(s):

- **Co-plan whenever possible**: In the rush of a school week, sometimes our planning isn't up to scratch. Sometimes we have crafted a masterpiece! Either way, share it with your teaching assistant. Seek their opinion and their critique. Ensure that they understand their role.

- **SEN and a shared responsibility**: Too often, teachers simply let teaching assistants sit with students with SEN like Velcro. Yes, some students are *statemented* for specific support, but, even then, you should utilise the opportunity to work closely with that student and expect the teaching assistant to work with and monitor other students.

- **Gifted and talented student support**: It is a peculiarity of our school system that we focus much of our money and attention on one end of the learning spectrum. Ask yourself how the teaching assistant could help challenge the most able students in the classroom.

- **Reading role models**: One of our core purposes is to promote and celebrate reading and all of its attendant benefits. We should, therefore, take every opportunity for all the adults leading the learning to share in the pleasure of reading. Involve your teaching assistants whenever you can.

- **Lead the learning together**: You should take every opportunity to ask your teaching assistant questions about how specific students are progressing, seeking feedback and generally seeking their opinion and promoting their opinion. Students remember when adults share their positive experiences of reading and writing, so explore the opportunity to do so.

- **Working with small intervention groups**: This can be undertaken within class and without. It should never be about simply removing challenging students. The teaching assistant should have a crystal-clear understanding of the task and the expectations for each student.

- **Feedback**: You should make obvious the feedback about individuals or groups in the class. Talking about how students have undertaken their task can be an opportunity for you all to celebrate progress or to reiterate expectations. Again, involve teaching assistants in feeding back upon exemplar answers, noting patterns, building upon your own feedback, etc.

- **Position in the plenary**: Often, teaching assistants are in an ideal position to evaluate and comment upon the progress made in the lesson. They can observe specific students who you have identified at the outset, or make more general observations.

If you have more than one teaching assistant, it may well reflect the complex nature of the group. If that is the case, then co-planning and more regular meetings may well be the order of the day. You are able to differentiate by grouping given that situation, and producing more overtly personalised resources may well become a viable option, or even a necessity.

On a human level, really get to know your teaching assistants. And remember, they may well be your saviours when you most need it.

ACTIVITY

You are teaching a group of eight Year 8 SEN students. They all have complex needs, and you have two teaching assistants. Your focus for the year is improving their functional writing and encouraging them to use reading strategies to read more independently.

- What would be the best grouping arrangement in the class? Would you have different arrangements for different tasks?
- How would you ensure your teaching assistants play a purposeful role in supporting all students, even though they may be allocated for the support of two particular students?
- How would you differentiate by your instruction to ensure they build their basic writing skills?

- What would you read with the group? What would be the typical duration of the reading? How would you get them to employ reading strategies successfully?

CASE STUDIES

Differentiation for SEN students

So, picture the scene: it's Day One of my NQT year and I am faced with a mixed ability Y8 class. In pairs, I ask students to discuss a book that they love; whether it be one they are currently reading or a childhood favourite. During feedback, Darren is still struggling to name a book. With a bit of prompting, he yells *James and the Giant Peach*! Jean-Louis, sitting next to him, merely wrinkles his nose and declares, 'I've just finished reading the works of Sartre. In French'.

It was clear that just 'pitching it to the middle' would not be sufficient, so here's a few strategies that my more experienced colleagues suggested:

- Differentiation by questioning: Design worksheets where the first few questions are straightforward, direct and accessible to all. Questions or tasks then become increasingly open-ended, complex and challenging.
- Alternatively, design different worksheets for different students, depending on ability. Tasks aimed at SEN students can be scaffolded, and less complex vocabulary employed.
- Differentiation when it comes to discussion can be tricky. My department have tried a 'No-hands-up' policy and instead draw lolly sticks, each with a child's name on, from a bag. This way, every child has to be ready with an answer and be an 'active learner'. This creates problems when the

question is difficult and the student randomly selected is not able to answer. **Tip**: Have two bags rather than one and draw from the 'most able' bag when the question is challenging. Alternatively, have 'hands up' for the most complex questions only.

- Use of teaching assistants: Your TA can be directed to work in class supporting students such as Darren, but it's a good idea sometimes to let the Jean-Louis types get some special attention too. Just make sure your TA is prepared beforehand and has had the chance to brush up on their Sartre!

Differentiation for English as an additional language (EAL) Students

I decided to try something a little different with my Y10s before starting work on *Great Expectations*. I took ten descriptions from the opening chapter and called one person up from every group to view the quotations for ten seconds only, before they reported back on what they had read. The challenge then was for the group to draw what their delegate had described.

During the judging of their work later, I saw a number of impressive churchyards, overgrown with nettles, and angry red lines depicting the sky. One group, comprised of three EAL students, had drawn a beautiful apartment block, standing all alone in the picture, bar its own sinister-looking shadow. When I pointed out that the marshland in Pip's time was unlikely to contain such architecture and pondered which quotation could have possibly given them this idea, Sohail exclaimed, 'Miss! It's a dark *flat* wilderness'.

- Always teach key terms and vocabulary. Don't assume, as I did, that they will be aware of alternative meanings to words. Asking them to draw what they have read, like the activity described above, is preferable for the very weakest when basic vocabulary is still being learned. Projecting pictures next to key vocabulary on the interactive board is also a useful tool.

- Use talk partners and sympathetically arranged groups for discussion. Students will feel more confident if they have had the opportunity to discuss ideas first, rather than responding directly to the teacher. By socially engineering partners and even groups, a mix of ability can be very successful. **Tip**: Try putting EAL students working at level 3a with those working at 5c. This can boost the confidence of the whole group, as your level 5s are likely to lead, and your level 3s will benefit from exposure to the vocabulary used by the other students, without being intimidated by those who may be working at top 5s and 6s in your class.
- Remember, SEN students will benefit from these strategies too.
- May your expectations be great!

Rachel Galletly, Assistant Subject Leader of English

TALKING POINTS

- What provision for SEN/EAL students does your school already provide?
- What information do you need to know? Who are the people in school that can support you? Who is the school SENCO?
- How does the grouping of classes in your English department impact upon differentiation?
- What are the unique ranges of needs in each class you teach? Are there common patterns?

Note

1 These mats don't confer independence for all students. Most, if not all, of the areas for support need direct teaching to illuminate the mat as a tool for proofreading or self-assessment, etc.

6 Using language to explain, question and feed back

Teaching may sometimes feel mystifying and too complex a task to quickly master for someone newly embarking upon the craft. From the mass of directives from Ofsted, to the many brilliant tomes of educational excellence for sale, there is a veritable smorgasbord of teaching strategies to choose from.

The mere mention of Ofsted can create unstoppable hysteria among even the most experienced of teachers and successful schools. It shouldn't. We should remember that the essential elements of great teaching do not require flashy technology, glossy labels or teaching packs – just skilled, well-practised pedagogy. The core essentials are as simple as 'one, two, three':

- Explain tasks and instructions with clarity.

- Question students effectively.

- Give well-judged feedback to students (formative assessment).

Now, each core aspect of this holy trinity of pedagogy has a great deal of complexity. This chapter will hopefully give you a toolbox of accessible tips to secure these core components of great teaching and learning.

Effective teacher talk is at once clear, supporting, directive and positive; it scaffolds understanding, elicits deep thinking, provokes challenging questions, and much more.

Sounds impossible? Don't panic. This complex language can be learned, it can be observed and it can be developed through deliberate practice. This chapter will hopefully draw back the veil from the mystery that is teacher talk and give you the confidence to undertake such talk like a seasoned pro.

Using language to explain

Step 1: What do students know and what do they need to know?

First, let's put the horse firmly in front of the cart: any clear explanation requires a good understanding of what your students already know.

Sometimes, that can include an in-depth, individual knowledge of little James and his love of Harry Potter, as well as his aversion to using punctuation accurately. It could encompass a good working knowledge of what a GCSE student beginning the course *should* know about essay writing. Having as much good information about what students know as possible adds to the quality and clarity of your instructions.

Vygotsky's concept of the ZPD of students is once again helpful. Effectively, you need to know at what level you should pitch your explanations.

You should therefore ask:

- What prior knowledge do the students already possess?
- How can I make this explanation intelligible and clear, but also challenging?
- What is the *core message* I want students to remember?

For example, if you were going to teach complex sentence structures to a Year 7 class, as part of a scheme of learning based around narrative writing, you would need to know if the students had a working knowledge of independent and dependent clauses. If they didn't, or if many struggled to remember these terms, then using them in your explanation would prove problematic. Ambiguity obviously hampers understanding.

The answer is, therefore, to arm ourselves with as much rich information about our students as possible: from summative and formative data, prior work and/or oral feedback, etc. We may then tentatively form conclusions about the best language to use. We should be able to differentiate it appropriately and pitch it at a level that is right – with enough challenge to move their learning forward. We need to ensure that there is enough familiar language to make learning accessible.

We also need to introduce challenging new vocabulary, with a clear explanation. So, know what the key terms are that you will want to use in the lesson and prepare to use them explicitly and even a bit repetitively. The idea, after all, is to hammer home the terms that will help your students understand the topic with confidence.

Step 2: Use patterns of challenging, subject-specific language

In most explanations, there are one or two key words that you want to stick in the minds of students. For example, if I were teaching my KS3 class Shakespeare and comparing *Romeo and Juliet* and the Sonnets, for example, subject-specific words would litter my explanations – literary terms such as *'hyperbole'* or *'iambic pentameter'*. We would explore the etymology of such words, explore linked vocabulary, analyse examples and repeatedly model them in our writing. With regular repetition, such key words become the touchstones of effective explanations. To make our meaning explicitly clear, we would stress these words in our delivery for explicit emphasis.

So, in class, my explanation might go something like this:

Good morning. Today we are going to learn about the most important literary term in the world – hyperbole. Some of you may already realise how hilarious that previous sentence actually was. Thank you for smiling Darren, you clearly appreciate wit when your hear it.

I'm sure Darren already knows that the term hyperbole is from an ancient Greek term *hyperbole*, meaning excess or exaggeration. The 'hyper' means 'beyond', followed by 'bole', which means 'a throwing action'. This gives us a nice visual of Romeo throwing his words beyond the actual reality [a physical demonstration may be apt]. Later in the play, he will talk about love jumping over walls, so hyperbole clearly is closely related to the language of love.

Now, Romeo, as we have established, is a little bit of a love-sick sonneteer himself. He just loves to talk about, well, love. Hyperbole is one of his key tools to crank up the emotion of his language and grab the attention of his potential ladies . . . [Note: with new terms and etymology, it pays to have students note down the essential information in their books, so they can revisit when required].

Step 3: Convey a clear core message

Notice what I'm not saying, *that most students struggle to learn anything*. But we are all programmed to be forgetful. Great teachers help build our vocabulary. Effective explanations, therefore, need to have the power of compressed language.

A good proverb, such as 'people in glass houses shouldn't throw stones', has an enduring power. It generates ideas, sparks connections and combines both easily digestible language and memorable imagery. We should aim to make our explanations have the memorable power of the proverb.

I would argue that most extended explanations could be compressed into such a memorable statement – the *core message* we want students to retain in their long-term memory. Most of this core knowledge is linked inextricably to the language of the lesson objective.

A great explanation may use the famous 'inverted pyramid', used by journalists to prioritise key information, which conveys the core message, at the beginning of the piece. Conversely, you may delay the core message until the end, building something like suspense. Whatever way you devise your explanation, be mindful of the *core message*.

Here is an example of a short explanation to an A level group, based on narrative style in *The Great Gatsby*, which homes in on the core message:

> F. Scott Fitzgerald is often credited with writing the great American novel. *The Great Gatsby* is celebrated for encapsulating America in the 1920s: the parties, the wealth and excess and social divides that were slowly tearing away at the American dream. We will analyse the rich language of the novel in great detail. The metaphors and imagery Fitzgerald uses are truly memorable. Perhaps the characters stand out the most. Gatsby is central, of course, but we must shine a light on the **narrator** – Nick Carraway.
>
> Our primary focus will be on the **narrative style** employed by Fitzgerald. From the opening page, we are introduced to the narrator, Nick Carraway. Every detail of the novel is carefully crafted through the tinted lens of Nick's opinions, morality and unconscious desires. He is perhaps the most famous **unreliable first-person narrator** of them all. For this reason we must analyse the **narrative style** and its subtle and nuanced impact on the reader.

Key terms are repeated. Important details – such as the key character who relates to the core message about narrative style – Nick – are made explicit. Clearly, students need to pursue the evidence, but hopefully they are lured in by the introductory explanation.

Step 4: Speak to engage their hearts and minds

It sounds rather grand to speak of the *'heart'*, but we are English teachers, we can do that type of thing. We are even free to quote an apposite line from a sonnet for good measure. On a daily basis, we are looking to stimulate the brains of our students, but, as we know, our brain and our complex systems of memory and thought are entwined with our emotions. Neuroscience proves that, when our emotions are stimulated, we learn better, our memory system becomes more attuned and alert. Now, we need to avoid the crippling effects of fear and spark more positive emotions.

This is perhaps easily done when we are teaching heartfelt poetry, such as Seamus Heaney's 'Mid-term break' to our Year 9 class, or the tragedy of *Hamlet* to our A level classes; but we must also trigger emotional associations with the driest subjects imaginable. You are not teaching to divulge your biography, but you do want to use personal anecdotes that make the topic feel real and to add emotional depth, sometimes memorably so. I often explain to my GCSE students about how I feigned illness when I was due to do my GCSE speaking and listening assessment at school, owing to my awful nerves and no shortage of cowardice! It is a good icebreaker when introducing individual speaking and listening presentations. It can be memorable in a powerful way.

If you want to appeal to their minds, make them think differently; challenge their assumptions. Without looking to be a stand-up comedian, make them laugh. A gentle joke about the topic, or even related to one of the more self-assured students, will keep them switched on to your more academic information. Poking fun at young Tristan, because of his excessive hair styling, may well link seamlessly to an explanation of the pride of Achilles for example. Getting a balance right is key. We are not comedians, and any attempt to be so would likely distract from the *core message*. That does not mean we should not aim to give lively, memorable explanations.

As most charity advertisements will attest, individual stories that spark empathy and interest prove much more memorable than mass-scale problems or abstract concepts. Emotional and personal stories are memorable. I remember very little about GCSE chemistry, except the emotive story of Marie Curie. We need these examples to hook their hearts and minds on to the core knowledge we want them to remember in the long term.

Step 5: Use accessible analogies, visual metaphors or media

Avoid at all cost the dreaded *'death by PowerPoint'*, or whatever presentation application is in vogue. If you do use supporting technological presentations, limit the number of words and use images as mental stimuli. An intriguing image to exemplify an idea can complement your explanation, without wholly distracting from the content. Playing a YouTube video with no purpose, other than for comedy effect, may temporarily endear you, but they won't learn anything!

Once again, there is lots of evidence, supported by cognitive science studies, to prove that narratives and analogies help deepen understanding. We need to do more than entertain our students.

Our minds naturally draw upon *'schemas'* – a fancy psychology term to define the existing patterns of knowledge we have to help us learn new knowledge. A key way of making new knowledge memorable is to hook it into existing schemas. For example, if we were given something to eat that we had never eaten before, then we would draw upon our prior knowledge: 'this tastes like chicken!' They give students helpful templates to build upon their prior knowledge and allow students to make educated guesses.

We need to ask whether using images or videos hooks into what the students already know. Do they build their knowledge around a topic? Does a visual metaphor clarify or confuse?

To get students to engage and relate to what they know, you can use examples such as relating writing skills to toolkits, paragraphing structure to rooms in their house – the list is endless. You may wish to compare your training to a ship on a tempestuous sea right now! Don't worry – calm will follow the storm!

Step 6: Tell compelling stories

Dan Willingham, in his excellent book, *Why Don't Students Like School?*, explains that stories are 'psychologically privileged' in the human mind and memory. For English teachers, this strikes at the heart of what we believe about emotion, memory and learning. Memorable personal stories bring the subject to life and drench dry facts with meaning. 'Sixty-four per cent of students achieving an A grade in exams' is interesting, but not nearly as memorable as personal stories of individual students toiling to overcome tough circumstances to achieve an A grade.

Our minds are programmed to make narratives. Our hearts and minds are captured when a 'conflict' is posed involving characters. Our explanations, therefore, need to be built like narratives, complete with characters, conflicts and resolutions. Stories should help illuminate the core message. This is a privilege for any English teacher – we love telling a good story!

If we are to illuminate the potency of the American dream for Willy Loman in *Death of a Salesman*, then we could talk candidly about our childhood dreams. I would relate my near-desperate desire to play for Everton Football Club – thwarted, as I saw it, by my poor eyesight and cumbersome NHS glasses! Students are typically happy to share their own stories – oftentimes memorably so.

When talking to my students about the courage needed to give an oral presentation to the group, I don't simply give them guidance on how to perform. I always tell them my personal story from school about my awful talks on earthworms in Year 8 and cancer in Year 10 – both equally as dire as the other. I relate how frightened I was when I began teaching – having to act confidently to students, when I wanted to be swallowed whole by the carpet beneath me. I *then* give them guidance about *how* to act confidently, *how* to speak with clarity and expressiveness to engage the audience.

Step 7: Make abstract concepts concrete and real

Akin to story making and using effective imagery and analogies to illuminate information, we better remember concrete knowledge over abstract knowledge. We are hardwired to do this. From birth, our first words are inevitably concrete nouns and verbs to articulate basic needs, such as 'Dad' or 'ball'. Hopefully, you have remembered the proverb used in step 3: 'people in glass houses shouldn't throw stones'. This is a great example of an abstract idea being made concrete and memorable linguistically. Beyond using our targeted, subject-specific language, we should avoid too much abstract language or jargon. It is only likely to create confusion. Be clear and concrete where possible.

Step 8: Hone the tone of your explanation

As you will no doubt know, 'getting them to listen' is essential; otherwise, your erudite explanations will be useless. You need to capture the right tone of voice, but, crucially, you must also consider the grammar of your talk. You may want to hook them in with some exclamative statements, getting their juices flowing ('You may be thinking that Lady Macbeth is as crazy as a bag of ferrets at this point!'); you may then proceed with some conditional and tentative interrogative statements about the topic ('Could Lady Macbeth reflect wider negative social views about the dangers of women?').

Like an artful speech, we should consider our language. Soon enough, this process becomes natural, and we do it automatically in the classroom.

Crucially, however, if students are to listen, we need to speak with confidence and clarity.

Using language to explain, question and feed back

We should exude confidence in our body language and use of hand gestures. We may have physical positions of authority in the room that students expect you to speak from. You may want to surprise them by speaking from a less typical position. Either way, a no-nonsense approach is often required. We should aim to be confident, expressive and in complete control.

Step 9: Check understanding

One way to secure attention and to make any crucial modifications to our explanations is to ask targeted questions. By having a 'no hands up' approach (asking all of your questions by selecting individual students with precision), you can secure a higher degree of attention, as students do not know who will be selected to respond to the question. Importantly, they do need thinking time when put on the spot like this. If students expect to be questioned on a given explanation in a habitual way, they are more likely to listen with intent.

We may find that we need to recast or reiterate an aspect of our explanation . . . or worse, start afresh and having to repeat much of our explanation! Better that, than students simply not understand what we need them to learn.

Of course, students forget, which is only natural. We, therefore, need to regularly repeat our core message. Doing so concisely, two or three times in a given week with a group, is not some admission of failure, but instead it is a viable strategy to help them remember better.

ACTIVITY

Choose a topic, such as a novel you know well. Give an explanation of that topic. Aim the explanation at a group of eager Year 7 students.

120

- What is the core message of your explanation?
- How will you adapt your vocabulary to make your explanation clear?
- What aspects of your explanation will prove challenging?
- What stories, images or objects will illuminate your explanation?

Question students effectively

Asking great questions and eliciting effective answers is too often an overlooked aspect of being a great teacher. Reflecting upon the questions we ask is really essential in ensuring we help students make great progress in English. With any new knowledge that is shared in teacher explanations, it is essential to decipher whether students have understood by using targeted questioning.

First, we need to define the different question types that we need to apply:

Closed questions

These questions are what they say on the tin. They have a very limited number of potential responses – often a single, factual answer. For example, asking a student 'what is the family name of Juliet?' to elicit a simple factual answer about the Capulet family name. These questions may not spark profound insights, but they are important when you need to quickly 'take the temperature' of the class and the students' general knowledge. Such questions can also ensure that more students are included in the questioning process. They can be quick and very useful.

Open questions

These questions are simply integral to developing the under-standing of students in your English class. These questions most often require analysis, evaluation and synthesis. A question such as, 'why is the Capulet family name so important to Tybalt?' is clearly a good follow-up question to the preceding closed question. The question demands that students evaluate Tybalt's character and his reasoning, while making links to other characters, such as Juliet or Lord Capulet himself.

These two question types are part of the fundamental building blocks of understanding. The following techniques ensure your questioning has maximum effectiveness:

Thinking time

The quality of student responses can be transformed if they are simply given more time to consider their answer. Giving ten seconds, with the expectation of receiving an answer, needs to be habitually applied, so that students are clear that they *can* and *should* answer challenging questions. This greatly reduces the degree of '**I don't know**!' answers (ban these answers unequivocally from your English lessons!) and helps build their confidence. Come back to students who have offered limited responses; give them hints and prompts. Of course, '*think–pair–share*' works very well here too in scaffolding student answers.

Planning participation

It takes some time, but planning beforehand who will be ques-tioned can help you shape targeted, differentiated questions. You can adapt your questions to suit individual students and then anticipate whom best to question in a sequence. It is important that, over time, each student in your class responds to questions fully, so that you can know their progress with a real sense of accuracy, supplementing written marking.

Probing questioning

It is often the case that students give closed, limited answers to challenging open questions. It is about getting students to clarify their ideas and often elaborate on their stunted responses. The following sequence may be typical in this regard:

Teacher: Why does Lady Macbeth imagine spots of blood on her hands?

Student: She has lost it and gone mad!

Teacher: Yes, she is certainly breaking down mentally, but why spots of blood?

Student: Well, it reminds her of the blood on her hands from killing Banquo.

Teacher: Why has that made her go mad?

Student: She has been driven mad by guilt at killing her husband's loyal friend.

Pose–pause–pounce–bounce

This is a brilliantly simple but very important strategy to ensure that you get all students participating actively in the thinking and questioning process. First, you need to *pose* a clear question. The thinking time at the *pause* point is crucial. Then *pounce* on a targeted individual, before bouncing the question to another student. The *bounce* is also crucial in that, once again, students are expected to constructively build upon the ideas of one another, which gets students focused on a consistent basis when trained.

Students asking 'why' questions

So far, we have focused on the teacher leading questioning so that they can evaluate the knowledge of the students, particularly post-explanation. It is equally important that students ask good questions, so that we can better diagnose their knowledge and understanding. Students actually ask surprisingly few questions of the teacher in class. Research has outlined that it can take six to seven hours for a typical student to ask a single question in class.[1] We need to ensure that questioning is shared evenly around the class, and that time is given over for high-quality, deeper questioning and feedback.

We can encourage such questioning and ensure it develops in an effectively structured way. We can use scaffolds, such as question banks or question stems, such as, 'Can I explain why . . .?' or 'What is the relationship between . . .?', etc. We also know that much of the feedback students get is from peers, and so we must ensure that the quality of the questions they ask one another is high. If we can calibrate students to ask better questions, we will make them better learners.

Give well-judged feedback to students

A wealth of national and international research supports what all great teachers in the classroom know: feedback matters. Good-quality, timely feedback makes a huge difference to student progress. John Hattie, in his seminal synthesis of research (involving more than two hundred million students), *Visible Learning for Teachers*, identified feedback as one of the most significant factors impacting student achievement.

As explained in the **assessment** chapter (**Chapter 4**), feedback is closely aligned with formative assessment. Oral feedback is inextricably linked to effective explanations and well-formulated and targeted questioning. It makes learning and progress visible. It is crucial to create the conditions of learning where students openly seek feedback and don't feel inhibited by potentially exposing themselves as supposed failures. The language of feedback needs, therefore, to be focused on the task and be specific.

As with most learning, students need scaffolds to support their progress. English teachers need to utilise subtle language cues to guide students to an effective response, while clearly dealing with misnomers.

When questioning students following an explanation, you need to be clear about the depth and scope of the feedback that you want to elicit. Sometimes, declarative facts are examples of feedback from students that identify the basic, but essential, knowledge that is required of students. Here are two examples of such closed questions that show a knowledgeable grasp of the content (these questions are based on a reading of *Of Mice and Men*, by John Steinbeck):

- **Closed questioning:**

  - *Teacher question*: 'What is foreboding?'

  - *Student answer*: 'It is when the writer hints at negative events to come.'

- **Closed, 'hinge' questioning:**

  - *Teacher question*: 'Which character suffers from the negative effects of racial segregation? (a) Crooks, (b) Curley, (c) Candy, (d) Carlson.'

  - *Student answer*: '(a) Crooks.'

These questions have the benefit of being concise and clear (and typically quick). They can be used to get direct feedback from an entire class. By using small whiteboards, quick questionnaires indicated by hand gestures, etc., we can identify if students have selected the core factual knowledge they need from the explanation. Our feedback is typically limited in this instance, but the next, obvious step is to ask our own 'why' questions.

With more open questioning, the teacher can then probe further to analyse whether students know and understand why such factual answers are right or wrong. Here are two examples of open questions that elicit answers which require elaboration:

- **Open questions:**

  - *Teacher question*: 'Which characters suffer the greatest degree of loneliness in *Of Mice and Men* and why?'

Using language to explain, question and feed back

- *Student answer*: 'I think that Crooks is the loneliest character because he is physically, mentally and emotionally separated from the other men. There is only one other African American family in Soledad therefore he can never really establish a range of lasting friendships.'

- **Open, 'hinge' questions**:

  - *Teacher question*: 'Which character suffers from the greatest degree of loneliness? Be prepared to justify your assertion and compare characters (a) to (d): (a) Crooks, (b) Curley's wife, (c) Candy, (d) George.'

  - *Student answer*: 'I would choose (d) George, because once he kills Lennie he will forever be living with his guilt and will no longer be able to develop friendships without thinking of Lennie. This loneliness will be worse than Crooks because . . .'

By thinking carefully about asking the right questions, we will have a better chance of getting the effective feedback we need to then move the learning forward. Often, students require small verbal prompts to ensure they elaborate upon their answers, such as 'explain further', 'tell me more about why you think that'. Or we can support students by asking them to make further relational connections that exhibit student understanding, such as, 'which character is . . . most like?' or 'consider the opposite viewpoint to the one you have just given'.

Do offer structural scaffolds that demand extra feedback, so you can be clear about their exact level of understanding. A quick verbal prompt may be as simple as 'and . . .', or other probing discourse markers, 'furthermore . . .', or, if you are digging for a counter-argument, 'in contrast . . .'. You can create a small concert of feedback by developing an oral response using typical discourse markers that initiate the 'bounce' to another student. Little Tim begins with the prompt 'first . . .', before you prompt Lucy with 'second . . .', and so on.

Many students have a default option of giving the shortest answer possible. Give them *wait time* (make this a habit, so that it is not unnecessarily uncomfortable). If they are genuinely struggling, then offer them a couple of alternative answers, or say that you are going to come back to them.

Once other students have fed back their views, you can return to the student who had initially failed to give an adequate response and probe them further. At the very least, they can judge responses that have been given by others, if they still cannot offer a developed personal response to the question posed.

CASE STUDY: ELASTIC EXPLANATIONS

To explain the concept of tension in novels, I take one thick elastic band. Always go for a thick band, as it inflicts more pain, and so students can see the band at the back of the classroom. Then I ask a student to hold on to one end of the band, while I simply hold the other end.

Step 1: Stand very close to the student and ask them to let go of the band. Nothing. The class ends up being very, very, very disappointed that no pain was inflicted on their dear teacher.

Teacher: Why wasn't that tense?
Student: Well, I knew it wouldn't hurt you at that distance, so I wasn't that interested.

Step 2: Stand about a metre from the student, holding the band. Give a nice dramatic pause when doing this and ask the student to let go.

Teacher: Why was that more tense than the last time?
Student: I thought that would really hurt you and I thought you'd chicken out doing it.

Using language to explain, question and feed back

Step 3: Stand as far away from the student as the band will allow you to. Then, move close to the student. Move away. Finally, move closer.

Teacher: How did I create tension there?

Student: I thought that one of you would let go and you'd be in pain, but then you moved and I relaxed a bit.

Step 4: Stand as far away from the student as the band will allow you to. Then, ask the student to . . . let . . . go at an unpredictable time.

Teacher: What caused the tension there?

Student: Seeing if he was brave enough to do it and seeing if you'd let him do it. Bet it hurt, sir!

Teacher: [whimpering] So, how does this link to the tension in our novel?

**Chris Curtis, English Teacher
and Literacy Coordinator**

CASE STUDY: ILLUMINATING EMPATHY

To explain the concept of empathy in *Of Mice and Men* and how Steinbeck masterfully manipulates the readers' attitudes and feelings towards Curley's wife, I used a Stanislavski belief exercise, or the 'little bird' belief exercise:

1   I folded an origami chick. I hid it out of sight.
2   As the students entered the room, I told them I needed to share something personal with them that had happened that morning.

I told them that, when I was taking the kids to the childminder, we had to stop the car because a bird had fallen from a nest.

My children demanded we stop. I flashed a couple of pictures of my kids on the screen.

3   I then said we hadn't time to get to the vet, so I'd brought the baby bird with me. I retrieved the 'bird'. I cradled it in my hands and held it close, then gradually showed them the 'bird'. I was met with bemusement and laughter.

It's important that you show that you completely believe at this point. I shushed them and told them they needed to be silent for the frightened bird. I invited them closer.

4   I asked them what they thought we should do. They responded with some silly answers, but mostly suggestions such as, feed it and, crucially, give it a name. During this time, it is really important to reprimand those who seem to be resisting the belief. They do fall into line if you maintain belief.

5   It was at this point that I stood up quickly from the chair where I was sitting quietly with the 'bird', before crushing it and putting it in the bin – 'killing' the bird.

There was shock and some laughter and lots of questions about why I'd do that. Many of them were genuinely shocked that I could do that to the creature that we had named.

I asked them why we had done what we had just done. They immediately went to Curley's wife and the lack of empathy we experience for her. They linked her to the baby bird. They considered the bird in the barn after her death. They considered the fact that Steinbeck gives us even more of her after she is killed than we get at any point before, making her death even more tragic.

The full text can be found at: http://creativeteachersupport.wordpress.com/2012/10/21/baby-bird/

**Gordon Baillie, Assistant Head Teacher
and English Teacher**

> ## TALKING POINTS
>
> - Did you experience any memorable explanations from a school teacher or lecturers? What features of style and content were particularly memorable? What can you learn from this?
> - What explanations are your students most likely to struggle to understand, and why? How can you combat this?
> - What types of question do you *typically* ask of students? How will you adapt your questioning style to be more effective in your English lessons?

Note

1   Graesser, A. C., and Person, N. K. (1994) 'Question asking during tutoring', *American Educational Research Journal*, 31(1), 104–37.

7 Ensuring good behaviour

If there is a chapter a trainee teacher will likely invest the most emotional energy reading, then it is this chapter on behaviour – based on sheer anxiety alone! No other subject quite has the 'wake up in the middle of the night fear' like the thought of being at the head of a class that you cannot control.

Those adverts about teaching, where students are singularly inspired to new heights by their invariably attractive and stylish teacher, don't ever depict the reality of life as a novice teacher (I can confirm I was no style icon!). It can be tough, but ensuring good behaviour is achievable, with firm and consistent behaviour management strategies and with support from your colleagues.

The predominant emotion of a new English teacher, alongside the driving excitement, is fear. The paralysing fear that, any moment, the group of gnarly teenagers before you might rebel into some united force – like a Roman phalanx of indifference. Thankfully, however, the emotion of fear is dulled by repetition. Those niggling devils that beset your thoughts become lessened. Students typically begin to learn more in your lessons than you do.

It is a question of character: like the qualities of a classical hero (I mean to select this rather grand analogy hopefully omitting the fatal flaw), a new teacher managing a class needs courage, resilience and persistence.

Ensuring good behaviour

Even the most experienced teacher has vivid memories of their first steps in quelling an unruly class – it can be a rather intimidating battle – but, if you don't win the battle, then you will not last in the classroom. I don't mean the phoney war of when you are undertaking your first lessons with observers present (most often an already experienced classroom teacher), but those lessons when you have sole responsibility for the learning of nearly thirty baying teenagers for an hour . . . a whole hour!

I'm afraid I cannot impart a simple, effortless answer, except that, with hard work, determination and support, *any* class can be whipped into shape. Some cynics debate this and will give you grizzly exemplars of such unteachable groups, but I do believe that the teacher can master any group, with skill and the required support from your school.

So, what are the keys steps to great student behaviour for the aspiring English teacher?

Q: What is the best behavioural management technique?

A: Teaching great lessons.

Great pedagogy is ultimately the best answer for the behaviour management conundrum. It is common sense really: students will behave better, the more they are engaged with their learning. With this simple but powerful knowledge, we must reflect upon behaviour in relation to our pedagogy, our planning *and* our behaviour management strategies.

All that being said, you may find yourself teaching the perfect lesson plan, superbly crafted and differentiated to meet the complex needs of each student . . . that falls completely flat because the students are simply not behaving. This is where your behaviour management strategies become so essential.

The reality is there is no quick-fix formula – otherwise that book would be an instant best-seller – but there are expert strategies you can implement and habits you can establish with students that make all the difference.

Teaching exciting, creative and engaging activities in your English lessons will no doubt do wonders for your behaviour management. Yet, there is an unsaid truth among teachers that some lessons are inherently a bit dull, no matter how you attempt to jazz them up, and so you can't always have students swept up in their learning to the point where their behaviour is impeccable.

Some skills, such as proofreading, just don't exercise the emotion of students to readily engage them.

You must, therefore, help students build good habits (often unnatural in a world that offers the instant gratification of a thousand television channels) and build *their* resilience in the face of what we might simply call *hard work.*

Habits take time to form: they typically take *relentless and rigorous routines.* Establish your routines, apply them fairly, and the students will fall into line – some more quickly than others, of course.

New and trainee teachers get a lot of advice about behaviour – so much so it can be somewhat dizzying and even plain confusing at times. The trick is to take on board the advice and to square that advice with the existing behaviour management systems in your school. Students are familiar with these habits and will expect to see you implement them, consistently and fairly – they will let you know in no uncertain terms if you don't.

Then, you must find a system you are comfortable with – implementing that system with the utmost rigour and consistency – every lesson, no matter how exhausting. Sometimes, you will be sorely tempted to let some small misbehaviours pass – perhaps, in the main, the group are working fine, it won't do you harm, you reason to yourself – but it undoubtedly will. Students are like elephants that never forget.

Consistency is king: create good habits and hold on to them like a dog with severe lockjaw.

Expert English teachers: what they do and say to command good behaviour

It can be infuriating at times to observe an expert teacher, with few easily discernible *special* behavioural strategies, control a class with seeming effortlessness. Sometimes, it is the self-same class that regularly leads you a merry dance. Even some of those students with hardened reputations who send shock waves of dissatisfaction through staffrooms appear to easily fall into line and lap up the learning for these expert teachers.

So, what do they do and say that makes the crucial difference? It certainly isn't effortless. It is a hard-earned skill; it involves developing a strong reputation and exercising regular habits with unflagging determination.

Undoubtedly, students recognise when a teacher has been at a school for a period of time. They also recognise status with a keen eye worthy of a bird of prey. I remember my time at school. My friends and I were like a pack of vultures when a prospective trainee teacher joined the fray. Students smell weakness: they pick up the scent of inexperience. This is an undoubted truth; however, in my experience, students are also democratic and fair, in that they size up a teacher first, giving them the benefit of the doubt before they form a judgement.

Akin to any animal pack, they want to see some confident leadership, some *dominant* behaviour to earn their respect. So, you need to exhibit confidence (even if you are really quaking in your school shoes) and unleash those skills of the *expert* English teacher.

Step 1: Speak with command

Sounds obvious, you say – well, yes, it is obvious. Speak with command and students will behave better. What is important is to know what that command sounds and feels like, to understand the nuances of the teacher talk that ultimately will keep students behaving appropriately and, therefore, learning as they should.

First, your *tone of voice* conveys a lot about you as a teacher. You don't need to shout incessantly – in fact, shouting invariably sends a message to students that you are not in control. You need a *range* in your tone and volume when you speak. Some teachers can get quieter and quieter in volume, but leave little ambiguity regarding their command of the situation and their feeling of annoyance.

Some teachers merely raise their hand and tap on a desk to gain total control, but, crucially, these signals are developed and used habitually. It may have taken a hundred repeated attempts before students knew implicitly what the desk tap meant.

Don't forget the power of *silence.* Many a new teacher has balked with fear at the idea of waiting silently for students to listen, but this habit can really establish control. Use little micro-signals, such as having a usual spot for where you require attention and silence, or have a physical signal, such as the aforementioned raising of your hand.

If you cannot get students to *actively* listen, then every subsequent attempt to teach the class will be potentially flawed – so persevere, with relentless effort. The following steps will help you establish that all-important *active listening* (see Scenario 1, p. 143).

Step 2: Speak with explicit clarity – leave no wiggle room

Crucially, the style of your language will convey command and erase any ambiguity about your intent for students. Sometimes, poor behaviour results from confusing, ambiguous instructions.

If you are desiring students to think creatively in response to a character in a novel, for example, you may wish to use '*conditional*' questions, such as, '*Could* you think of the dominant feelings Macbeth is experiencing here?'. Yet, if you are attempting to give clear commands about behaviour or task setting, then 'conditional' instruction can sound the death knell for your degree of command. Rather than '*Please could* you work in silence?', you need a commanding imperative, with a clear stress upon key words, for instance, 'I *want* **independent** writing – **in silence** – **no** speaking to others – for **any** reason. **Do** we understand?'. Clear, unambiguous, with no wiggle room. The tag question at the end of the imperative further reinforces your point, giving students some feeling of choice, when in reality you are in complete command. You can always soften your tone when you have a group firmly in hand.

Over time, you want to shorten your commands, so that students waste no time in interpretation. With relentless repetition, 'independent writing' can be a command that represents a whole host of micro-behaviours you expect students to exhibit.

Consider: What are the short-hand phrases you need to develop to convey command? When you observe experienced teachers, what phrases and commands do they habitually use?

The best teachers are crystal clear in their instructions and in their method. Precise choices in your language use are obviously crucial.

Expert teachers also have their own clear system of behaviour management. There is no right or wrong here, within reason. The answer is simply whatever warning system is clear and fair and eliminates wiggle room. It also needs to be in tune with your school's systems, so that students are familiar with it.

My method of behaviour management is a simple warning system, used ever since I was a cowering NQT. It is wholly unoriginal, but effective in its clarity and simple steps, while being in sync with the school behaviour management system:

- **Verbal warning**: This may be for talking when they shouldn't, distracting others, chewing or other such low-level examples of misbehaviour. Quick. Decisive. On record.

- **Take their student planner, placing it on the teacher's desk, and warn them that they face a bad comment at the next step:** This clearly fits in with our school-planner system. It can be done discreetly if you do not want to disturb the class. It can be done very publicly, as a wider warning to the group.

- **Write a bad comment in their planner**: At my school, parents sign planners; form tutors and heads of house check planners. This means the planner has power. Follow whatever system that you know utilises the support structures of your school pastoral system.

- **If they continue to misbehave, set a detention**: The topic of detentions is contentious. Some respected behaviour experts decry them. I think they are useful in establishing your status and provide a useful sanction. They need to be followed through. If students know you will not punish non-attendance, well, they won't attend! Be rigorous and relentless about detentions. They are time-consuming and difficult. But, in my experience, you will soon find that the volume of your detentions decreases over the course of the year. They shouldn't be used indiscriminately, but they are a very useful sanction.

- **If they are being directly rude or objectionable, immediately follow this up with the appropriate figures in the school hierarchy after the lesson**: Some new teachers fear looking powerless by seeking support. Remove this concern. It is both responsible and practical to seek such support. Good school systems will encourage this to occur.

- **In the case of a serious refusal or act of misbehaviour, such as a fight, I would send an urgent note with a reliable student to my subject leader, or the on-call senior leader, to remove the student**. There are, hopefully rare, extreme examples of misbehaviour. They happen in every teacher's class at some point. If one occurs in yours, act swiftly and confidently to seek support.

This system might seem very straightforward. I would hope so. It is meant to be a simple, step-by-step process every student needs to understand; it is an escalator students know they shouldn't walk up, but still attempt to do so on a near daily basis.

Some teachers disagree with the concept of detentions. In my experience, they are a useful sanction that you will end up using less and less. Still, it is an important tool – particularly if it is an expectation in your school behaviour management system. You can actually develop positive relationships and get some valuable learning done in this time.

Your school may not run a system with planners and comments. Not to worry; they will have a system. Stick to it. Make students know that you know it like your date of birth.

Step 3: Ensure students know what good behaviour looks and feels like

Too often, teaching professionals forget the fact that they have a whole host of established habits that made them good learners and successful at school and in their subsequent careers. It is the *curse of the expert*.

Ask yourself the simple question: 'Does Jimmy understand what the appropriate behaviour is in your English class?'. Don't make assumptions. Instead, ensure students *learn how* to behave and have it *reiterated* on a regular basis. Think: what exact behaviours do you expect? It requires some thought.

With any new group, I ensure they know how to learn, before we embark on our English curriculum. Many students simply do not know what being a good learner *feels like* or what a good learner *looks like* at work, or even *how* to become any better. We need to help them learn good behaviours for learning, as much as we need to help them learn to write and write with skill.

We confidently talk to them about becoming '*independent learners*', but have you had students collaborate to try to unpick what we mean by an 'independent learner'? If you have, is it memorable or visible in the classroom?

A good task to undertake is to have students work in groups to create '*the ideal English student*'. They can have fun creating a name – you can give them prompt questions as a starting point. At the heart of the task is getting students to unpick how to learn effectively. You can select the best character – with a composite of the best skills, attitude and qualities required. Have that character visible and on display in the classroom. Oh, and prepare for some *'geek'* stereotypes to challenge!

This can be referred to on a regular basis to reiterate the key messages about learning, while simultaneously providing a template for good behaviour in a very *positive* way. It creates a tacit set of expectations about how they need to learn in your classroom.

You can create 'class rules' based on this activity. You can establish behaviour for speaking and listening activities by referring to the 'ideal English student', and so on. Have the highest of expectations, but never assume students know intuitively what you expect.

Step 4: Set the tone early and be relentless about standards

With student behaviour, there is no doubt a *Pygmalion effect* at work – you will get what you expect most of the time. If you lower the standard, so that students can wriggle out of doing homework, then many of them won't do it, and standards will inevitably fall. If you expect students to have high standards for all their class work, then you need to put in the hard marking so that they continue to confer that high standard on to their work.

Ask yourself: What will you do if students complete substandard work? Will you ask them to redo the work? If so, how will you monitor that this task is completed to your satisfaction? Have a policy only to accept outstanding work. Show students what outstanding work looks like. Put in the effort to monitor in a register the completion and quality of their work.

Put simply, set the tone.

Remember, great pedagogy is the best behaviour management tool there is – that is why planning is essential to progress. If the standard of work slackens, then the behaviour will too, and vice versa.

Ensuring good behaviour

Don't accept substandard behaviour and don't accept substandard work. It can be gruelling, but making students redo work to an appropriate standard makes all the difference in setting the right tone and establishing your reputation.

Follow it through – bad behaviour, poor effort, or both: ring parents and liaise with your subject leader or the appropriate pastoral member of staff.

If you have higher standards for some students than others, then they will surely identify the unfairness with unerring accuracy and resent you with a force that could turn tides. Never, I repeat never, allow one student to move from your seating plan, or go the toilet, after you have denied others previously.

Consistency matters.

The most notorious of students are predictably more in need of high standards of behaviour than others, even if that means a challenging confrontation may be at hand. Be consistent and remember: high standards are absolutely essential.

Step 5: Be positive and reward good behaviour

Those teachers with the best behaviour management aren't always vicious fear-mongers – many have a quiet authority. I would suggest that *positive, assertive discipline* is the way forward.

I don't mean some laissez-faire, 'softly, softly' approach, where we thank students for simply doing as we ask at every stage, or pander to every whim and need; rather, focus on the positive. Be relentless about verbalising good behaviour or, 'excellent focus, Claire – pen down and listen, Georgina', etc.

Those *expert* English teachers mentioned at the start of the chapter do this instinctively and quickly all the time. It manifests in small moments in a lesson, such as:

- praising a student who is organised and ready to learn first: 'Well done Jimmy – ready and reading before others have taken off their coats';

- praising a student who has modelled good listening, as shown by his subtle response that developed upon an answer from another student: 'Lovely response Tom. James what do you think of that great idea?'.

This praise is personal and genuine – not saccharine or overdone. If the school has a reward system, such as good comments, the expert uses this system with skill. But, even more so, the expert builds up intrinsic motivation from his or her brethren. High standards can become habit. Students can be made to feel guilty and genuinely saddened if they are exempt from praise.

Let's face it, we all like to be liked and praised – students, with their delicate sense of their fledgling identity, feel this acutely – despite their often brilliant masking of the fact.

Step 6: Tweak the environment to improve behaviour

The key tweak is a crucial component of behaviour management – *the seating plan*. The importance of a seating plan cannot be understated with regards to establishing the right habits and atmosphere in your English classroom. From the very first lesson, knowing your students' habits and behaviours is key.

Seating arrangements can be refined, the more you know your group. From gender balance, to friendship groups and ability levels, there is a vast array of factors that can determine a good plan. Like most behaviour management, it takes some trial and error to work out which is best for you.

Take care of other small details: does your seating arrangement allow you fluid and effective movement about the room? Does your room set-up distract students or unnecessarily clutter the learning space? Are resources, such as paper, dictionaries, etc., easily accessible to minimise disruption.

Put simply, an ordered room can help foster an ordered atmosphere. All the small details matter. Sweat the detail.

Ensuring good behaviour

Many teachers do not have their own classroom base, and so forming solid and consistent habits of using any room space helps maintain your high standards. From room to room, try to maintain the same seating plans, the same orderly approach to entering the room, etc. If, as part of your typical pedagogical approach, you use a 'question wall', then move whatever you can to establish the same resource in each classroom you teach – even if it means using more temporary resources, such as post-it notes.

A physical control of the space is important too, as it conveys command. When the students enter the room, are you confidently welcoming them into your space? Are you conveying control by quickly asking them to remove bags? Are you circulating the room assertively? Are you asking students to get out folders, close windows, etc.?

Each small command can convey control. Like a hawk, you are ready – hovering in control – the whole classroom in the steady grasp of your (caring but forceful) talons.

Do you speak from a consistent spot in the room? Or do you change the dynamic by explaining from the back of the class?

Your physical movements matter.

A word of warning: don't hide behind the teacher's desk. Move about the room with a confident posture. It can help you diffuse little issues, such as tapping pens or chewing gum, and, most importantly, gives students the message that you control the classroom space.

Step 7: Follow the school systems with rigour

Ultimately, this whole chapter, and student behaviour more generally, is about key, simple messages. Build consistent habits for students and maintain those habits and standards relentlessly. The **three Rs** are: **relentless** and **rigorous routines**.

I have repeated the phrase in this chapter – you should repeat the ethos in your classroom. This applies to how you place yourself as a teacher within the hierarchy of the school. Despite some of the more hysterical reporting in some of our more vehement tabloids, many schools have strong systems for maintaining good behaviour.

When selecting your school, do ensure that the school has a clear and rigorous behaviour management system. The reality is that students are keenly aware of such whole-school systems, and they will live up, or live down, to the expectations of the school.

Do ensure that you follow the school rules, and students will respect you for it (perhaps after a period of resentment). As stated earlier, use the school reward system to focus on positive behaviour as much as you utilise the school system for punishment, if not more.

Behaviour scenarios

SCENARIO 1: YEAR 9 ENGLISH, START OF THE SCHOOL YEAR: LESSON 1

The opening lesson with any class pretty much integrates all of the aforementioned steps for taking command of behaviour in the classroom. Mr Jones always follows the same steps to quickly establish order and command.

- First, students are asked to stand in orderly lines outside the classroom, and then they are invited warmly into the classroom, before a projected image of the classroom seating plan guides them towards their seat. Mr Jones chooses to sit students boy–girl and in group tables at KS3. He spoke to the Year 8 teachers about his new group, as well as his subject leader, which gave him some hints about certain characters and some good groupings regarding friendship, while differentiating some students by ability to establish a good balance in the classroom.
- Second, Mr Jones has developed his own patter for introducing himself to new classes, balancing humour with assertive command:

Hello Year 9. As I am sure you already know, my name is Mr Jones. If I have taught you before then you will know the rumours are true – I am an ogre who demands perfect behaviour at all times! In all seriousness, I don't mind a joke when the time is right, but if we are all going to enjoy English and feel safe in our classroom we need to be really clear about how we behave and why that is so important. The first rule that is completely non-negotiable is that you must listen to me and other students in the class with your full attention, politeness and respect.

- Mr Jones then goes on to define what he means by *active listening with the class.* [**Active listening** can easily be defined as listening in a physically responsive way – eye contact and physical communication, such as appropriate nods, alongside appropriate verbal cues.] The phrase *active listening* becomes his key short-hand phrase for behavioural expectations. The group does a 'think–pair–share' response to the question: 'What does good active listening look and sound like in English?'. Mr Jones collates the best ideas by questioning the pairs on paper and retains the answers on the wall for a short time to reiterate the concept (these can be collated quickly, before making them visible in the classroom).

- To reinforce their understanding, Mr Jones has students work in trios to exchange interesting biographical information, for a quick *Just a minute* presentation on one other student from the trio. This nice introductory activity gives Mr Jones the chance to get to know the group more personally, while also celebrating good models of active listening, with a task that exemplifies why successful listening is so crucial.

Questions to consider in response to Scenario 1

- What routine will you establish in your first lesson with your groups? Will it alter depending upon the age, key stage or make-up of the group?
- What introductory speech will you make to your groups, and how will it set the tone?
- What are the key rules that you absolutely refuse to compromise upon?
- What good **learning** behaviours do you need to establish from the very start?

SCENARIO 2: YEAR 11 ENGLISH: A LESSON BASED ON PERFORMING INDIVIDUAL ORAL PRESENTATIONS

Ms Curry has a challenging Year 11 group that needs to complete more formal speaking and listening assessments. She anticipates that many of the group will struggle to be able to sustain their concentration for long periods.

- First, Ms Curry reiterates the importance of the speaking and listening assessment and why they have the capacity to be successful. She questions students about what relevance this skill of presenting to groups of people has for their future lives. She concludes by relating her personal story of how nervous she was when she had to complete a similar oral presentation when she studied for her English GCSE.
- Second, Ms Curry allows the group ten minutes to collate their materials and prepare for their prospective presentation (she refrained from giving them an order for who is presenting, in an attempt to create a state of continual 'readiness' and focus). It is made clear that they are not

allowed talk. If they have a question, they have to write it on a post-it note and place it on the board (allowing for a more discreet answer that doesn't disturb the class). When the ten minutes have passed, she offers students the chance to ask any questions they have. They then complete their preparations, with clear timings being indicated to keep them on task. Ms Curry supports some individuals where appropriate, ensuring she positions herself to have a full view of the class. Some students are warned to stay focused on the task.

- When the preparations have ended, Ms Curry reminds students that it is a speaking and *listening* assessment. She concisely reiterates what good *active listening* looks and sounds like, questioning students to reinforce her point. She then clarifies that students are expected to have a pen at hand at all times to make a note of relevant questions to ask of the student giving the presentation. Although not essential to effective questioning, Ms Curry wants students to focus on a task during each presentation to attempt to minimise their distractions.

- After calling the first student to perform (a confident student she knows will make a strong start), she asks that student whether they will benefit from the audience being supportive and focused – to which they agree – investing some emotional agreements between the students to engage their hearts and minds in the task.

- After the first presentation, she requests some students to ask questions by name, thereby establishing this pattern and helping to ensure that every student has to listen to every presentation.

- At the end of the lesson, Ms Curry celebrates the efforts of those presenting, while also focusing upon the quality questioning, due to the good behaviour and respect shown by students in the class.

Questions to consider in response to Scenario 2

- What running order is most appropriate for this particular group?
- Where will you position yourself to assess, but also monitor behaviour, effectively?
- How would you further engage the continued interest of the group in the breaks between presentations?

SCENARIO 3: YEAR 8 ENGLISH: SUPPORTING A RELUCTANT STUDENT WITH PERSISTENT BEHAVIOURAL ISSUES

Ms Welch teaches a student – we shall call him James – who is easily distracted, and he attempts to interrupt the lesson frequently. He often produces a poor standard of classwork, despite having sound literacy skills. The class more generally could be euphemistically described as 'lively' – James is often a key trigger for misbehaviour in the group, and he has a wider reputation in the school for poor behaviour. Ms Welch consistently applies the following approaches:

- James sits near the front of the class, in the seating place facing Ms Welch and the front of the class.
- James is most often seated next to a student of similar ability, usually a girl (they often have a magical effect in tempering the most reluctant of males!), whom he is encouraged to work with collaboratively and support where appropriate.
- Ms Welch makes a point to attempt to speak personally to every student in the class, every lesson. She most often greets James at the door and sizes up his current mood.

James is discreetly praised when he is focused on his work and working well.

- James, alongside the rest of the group, is reminded how the 'ideal English student' would learn and act in any given task. James is often asked to surmise how the 'ideal student' would perform.
- Ms Welch has established habits of focusing on positive learning behaviours (with some concerted resistance) by using the '**Secret teacher**' approach, for example, asking students, obviously including James quite often, to secretly monitor the learning of the class and nominate students to receive praise or a good comment, for excellent contributions to the learning.
- Ms Welch never allows James the oxygen of attention when he shouts out. She calmly uses micro-signals, such as putting her hand up to signal James to be quiet, or diffuses minor distracting behaviour, such as pen tapping, by subtly, but forcefully, placing his pen on the desk, not skipping a beat with her whole-class talk.
- Ms Welch never escalates the situation with James by shouting. She calmly, but forcefully, explains the consequences of his behaviour and each step of her behaviour management routine.
- Ms Welch does make time to discreetly explain to James that he isn't behaving as he can do, and she is always warm and disarming, often to James' dismay, as he would much prefer a good argument! She always aims to develop a positive relationship with all her students, particularly the most challenging. She goes out of her way to find out the personal circumstances of students, which informs her sensitive choice of language.
- Whenever James misses homework, forgets his book or misbehaves, Ms Welch is relentless in following through with sanctions. James knows she is consistent.

He complains he doesn't like her, but he certainly respects her authority.

- If James or anybody else misses a detention, Ms Welch pursues them with persistent energy – often ringing home to ask parents to support her in helping their child learn. Parents are almost always supportive, especially when you get in early, with less emotive issues.

Questions to consider in response to Scenario 3

- Who is the best person to know the latest information about James and other problematic students?
- Which teachers are most effective at teaching James, and why? Can you observe their practice?

TALKING POINTS

- Do you have a 'natural style' in the classroom? Will you need to adapt that style for different classes? Once again, can you identify your early strengths and areas to improve?
- What are the crucial steps in your whole-school behaviour system? How can you apply them fairly and consistently?

8 Dealing with observations

The real truth of observations is that those observing you most often already have a sound preconception of your skills, strengths and weaknesses. A one-off lesson will not make or break you and, therefore, consistency is king.

In many ways, the lesson observation is only a snapshot. If you have been teaching good lessons consistently, you need not worry so much about a one-off lesson. Students will have formed good habits and will respect your authority. Most typically, your students are rooting for you to do well.

Many times, as an English subject leader, I have observed new teachers (and experienced teachers, I might add) aim to present a showpiece lesson that has fallen flat on its face – rather inevitably – because no habits of the 'showpiece' had been established with students on a consistent basis.

So, remember the fundamentals of good teaching and good pedagogy. Teach lessons that stretch yourself and your students, but don't put on a showpiece that bears little resemblance to the weekly reality of your teaching practice and their learning.

A great question that Ofsted inspectors often ask students is this: 'Are your English lessons normally like this?'. It is the perfect question to validate great teachers who are committed to their craft on a daily basis, not just for one-off observations. If you are consistent, it will shine through. If you have developed positive relationships with students, it will shine through. If you are a good teacher, it will invariably shine through.

Ask yourself: what will be your *normal* approach to teaching English? Is it clear and effective?

Despite all that positive thinking, you may well be thinking that you *still* feel extra pressure to perform in an observation. You still feel under the microscope and that it is *different* to *normal* lessons. Indeed it is, but you need to keep it in perspective. It is important not to build up the observation psychologically into something that is potentially nerve shredding.

Remember: *Don't deliver the lesson to or for the observer!* You are teaching for your students. Focus on their learning, and everything else will follow.

Speak to colleagues – they have been through the same experience. Ask your mentor or a colleague you trust to talk through your lesson planning for tips and reassurance. Do what it takes to reduce your stress about that observation . . . within reason!

There are a few essential questions an observer will have in mind as they assess your teaching and the progress made by your students:

- Do the students have a clear understanding of what they need to learn?

- Do the students know how to improve?

- Are there appropriate opportunities for sharing new knowledge, practice and purposeful feedback with students, so that they can make progress in English?

Your lesson plan should competently address these questions.

Organise your resources and be prepared. Know the students; know what you want them to achieve. Craft a lesson around what you want them to learn and not around a 'fun' activity that may look ostensibly good for an observer in your English classroom.

Making sense of Ofsted

Ofsted inspectors are the *Ringwraiths* of education for many teachers. The mere mention of their presence makes normally rational adults weak with fear. For any English teacher, unpicking the vagaries of the Ofsted criteria is a useful activity. They are not a checklist to be ticked off in sequence, but they do present a common framework for English teachers.

The following is the supplementary subject-specific guidance for English,[1] based upon the criteria for 'outstanding' (let's aim for the stars). Even though the details may go out of date, the messages about what we typically consider as 'outstanding' teaching are long-standing.

Supplementary subject-specific guidance

Outstanding (1)

Pupils show high levels of achievement in the different areas of English (reading, writing, speaking and listening) and exhibit very positive attitudes towards the subject.

This guidance is pretty much common sense. The evidence of 'very positive attitudes' could comprise the buzz in the room during an activity, a willingness to contribute or conversation with the Ofsted inspector. 'High levels of achievement' will be patently evident in the quality of oral contributions and in students' books/folders.

Pupils rapidly acquire secure knowledge of letters and sounds and make sustained progress in learning to read fluently and with understanding.

This guidance clearly relates to reading. Reading 'fluently and with understanding' is a rather general phrase, but it would be clear in the teaching and learning that students have developed the reading skills to grapple with complex texts. Through high-quality teacher talk and student–teacher interactions, challenging vocabulary and concepts would be made clear and understandable. Once more, having a working knowledge of the ZPD of each student helps ensure that we provide them with the right reading materials to make 'sustained progress'.

> Pupils are very keen readers and show a sophisticated insight into a wide range of challenging texts, both traditional and contemporary.

A 'keen' attitude to reading may be evident in the ongoing work of students and in their verbal understanding. Progress would be relative here. With a Year 7 English group, students' knowledge of 'traditional' texts may be nascent at best, whereas other Year 7 students may have had a reading-rich upbringing that sees them excel beyond their peers. With a group undertaking English literature at A level, you would hope that the lifeblood of the lesson is suffused with a rich array of texts being referenced and studied. Being 'keen readers' is important. Has the classroom teacher promoted reading? Is time created to read purposefully? More broadly, this is also a whole-school challenge (as well as a wider cultural matter) regarding how we ensure reading for pleasure is alive and well in our English classrooms.

> Pupils' writing shows a high degree of technical accuracy and they write effectively across a range of genres, frequently showing creativity in their ideas and choice of language.

'Technical accuracy' will be unmistakably evident in the ongoing work of students that Ofsted may well choose to skim. It will also be clear in our pedagogical approach to writing. Teachers who embed proofreading and drafting skills into every writing task will see students exhibiting more 'effective' writing. The culture of crafting a piece of writing, both in terms of purpose and audience and with high levels of accuracy, does promote truly creative improvement in students' writing.

Dealing with observations

> Pupils have a mature understanding of the differences between written and spoken language. They speak confidently and with maturity, using Standard English very effectively when required.

This guidance refers to a sense of register, in both the written and the spoken mode, being evident in the teaching and learning. Successful English students understand the 'academic code' that applies to most writing and to many more formal opportunities for talk. In students' oral contributions and in the writing undertaken in the lesson, it will be evident that students can flexibly adapt their language with appropriateness. If we don't ensure they communicate with this degree of fluency, it will inhibit their writing and their ability to communicate in class and beyond.

> Pupils have learned to be effective independent learners, able to think for themselves and to provide leadership, while also being sensitive to the needs of others.

Our English students' being 'effective independent learners' is an outcome we would all wish for our students. In practical terms, it manifests itself in students being able to undertake a writing task and be imbued with the good habits of checking their own work, of working through issues with drafts, etc. It would be bolstered by support resources, such as dictionaries or writing mats, but, ultimately, having truly 'effective independent learners' requires a great deal of great teaching.

It may begin with a dependence upon teacher support, followed by the interdependence provided by modelling and scaffolded learning.

Independence is, therefore, a desired goal of our teaching. In some lessons it will be evident; in others, students will require more direct support. We should be wary of setting students off on a path to discovery that they are ill equipped to undertake. We should be flexible in our planning and teaching, giving students a balanced diet of teaching and learning.

Make yourself and your classroom observer ready

All our life, so far as it has definite form, is but a mass of habits.
(William James)

I will reiterate the value of consistency, effective routines and good habits. When you have worked hard at establishing routines and you see them flowering gradually, then an observation seems less of a frightening prospect.

Be yourself. Stick to your core routines and habits. Ask yourself: what are your core routines and habits? They may not be immediately apparent. Phone a friend; reflect on your practice.

Take some reasonable risks – it is a chance to learn and potentially make mistakes. You can always fare better next time. Most observations are a chance for you to develop your practice. More experienced teachers actually lose the valuable opportunity to receive feedback on their teaching that being a new teacher offers.

Some core habits of your teaching work alongside some common-sense tips regarding having an observer in your classroom:

- Before the lesson, whenever possible, ensure that each classroom is ready, with a good stock of paper or whatever resources you envision you may use.

- Don't commit a cardinal sin and focus the opening of your lesson on the needs of your observer rather than on those of your English class. Quickly greet your students and get them on task quickly with some 'bell work' (an activity designed to focus students quickly, *on the bell,* such as a reading activity or a 'big' question to answer). Then communicate with the person observing your lesson, if you need to do so.

- Prepare your room so your observer has a defined space. Consider sitting them next to students confident enough to communicate with an adult in such circumstances. Share any resources with your observer, so that you and they can simply focus on the lesson.

- Feel confident to refer to prior learning, including the students' letting the observer know what they have been working on in English, where appropriate.

- An observer may well speak to students about their progress. An important part of developing good learning habits is to ensure students can articulate what they are learning, why they are learning and for what purpose, and finally where they are likely going. An Ofsted-style question may well be 'what grade are you working at and how do you need to improve?'. This is a valid question that tests how well you have shared feedback with students.

- Don't be afraid to be politely assertive and to explain the rationale of your pedagogical decisions to your observer.

Most new teachers misapprehend that a lesson observation is all about them. It is not. It is ultimately about the students. Every observer will have at the forefront of their mind: are the students learning and making progress? Your teaching is all about planning to ensure this is happening, while responding flexibly when it isn't.

When making your lesson plan for an observer, consider isolating three different students in your planning. At each stage, consider whether each of those students is learning effectively and is engaging, and also factor in how you will *know* this is the case. It also has the benefit of making us all less self-obsessed about a lesson observation.

It isn't all about us. It may sound clichéd, but it is most definitely about the students.

Plan, with secure knowledge of the students that is shared with the observer

Our core business is to help our students learn to the very best of our ability. The purpose of observations can be to evaluate our practice, but any such evaluation is determined by how much students progress in a given lesson. With that in mind, we can plan for an observed lesson with progression explicit in our planning and the learning of our students.

It is good practice to identify individual students – ideally, students who span the ability range in the group – and pinpoint how they will exhibit progress in the lesson plan. You can identify those students in the lesson plan and share this information with the observer.

For example, if you target differentiated questions at those students, you can accurately pinpoint progress. Often, the difficult part is responding with timely and flexible adaptations to your plan.

Small details show you have a great knowledge of the students. Using their name is a prerequisite, but knowing their individual needs, strengths and weaknesses can be incredibly powerful when you are working with students or conducting whole-class feedback.

Take the presence of the observer as a well-deserved opportunity to celebrate the achievements of your students and reinforce your relationship with those students by showing you know just what they require to learn best.

Another solid indicator of both sound planning and excellent knowledge of your students is to present the observer with a well-considered seating plan. It may be that you deploy various seating plans depending on the lesson and the task (cleverly exhibiting your ability to differentiate once more), or that you have sat students in specific spots to get the chemistry of the group just right.

Be willing and confident in explaining your plans to the observer.

Sometimes, even for the most experienced of observers, watching a group can be deceptive. There are legions of little micro-behaviours that show that a group is really making great progress that aren't immediately discernible. Sometimes, that progress is relative to what has gone before. A difficult class being in good order may be a terrific success at the given stage of the observation.

The key is to make the progress visible to the observer. Get the students discussing productively, share best work in the plenary as a model of exemplary progress, and so on. Don't be afraid to set the observer straight about the group. Show them that you are a confident and effective English teacher.

Ensure students receive a 'balanced diet' of teaching and learning

Michael Wilshaw, erstwhile leader of Ofsted, the government inspectorate, has reiterated on more than one occasion that there is no prescribed method of teaching and learning that is best. Don't be seduced, magpie-like, by the latest shiny teaching gimmick. English teaching is awash with fads and fashions as much as any other profession or walk of life. Trying a new teaching strategy once is often a poor indicator. You need to practise and learn a teaching strategy for it to be really effective. In observations, ensure that you stick to your core routines for great learning.

Avoid using technology for the sake of it to impress an observer. I am not saying technology cannot help create outstanding learning. When it is rooted in sound pedagogy, it can be a great lever to engage students and deepen their learning. An observer may be impressed by students buzzing around the building with a fleet of tablet computers, but ensure you have a clear objective for what they are learning. Be prepared for the technology to go wrong – plan for an alternative.

There may well be no perfect lesson structure for us all to follow. That being said, starting with a compelling explanation, undertaking some modelling and shared practice, before moving towards some independent learning seems like a pretty common-sense formula.

Tie that up with a clear plenary that synthesises the learning and provides a clear map of where you are going and, not only will you likely tick the boxes of the observer, but also, more importantly, your students will learn well.

Don't be seduced by the fatal flaw of cramming too many activities into your lesson. Sometimes, students being busy, firing post-it notes around the room or revolving groups around the room every two minutes may appear to be *rapid progress*, but it doesn't make for deeper learning. Common sense tells us that rattling through a Shakespeare play at speed may well not help students understand it better.

You will quickly learn the difference between 'rapid' activities and 'rapid' learning. Such learning motors along speedily because explanations were clear, modelling was instructive, etc. It is not because the students were out of their seats every five minutes, looking busy.

Sometimes, deep, considered discussion is required. The teacher may need to reiterate essential points. Students may well have to rewrite or redraft their work with a painstaking sense of difficulty. Often, the deepest understanding comes from slow, thoughtful learning. Beware the false idol of *rapid progress*.

Don't panic if the lesson goes off piste!

A key differentiating factor between a novice teacher and an expert teacher is the capacity to deal with the immediate challenges of a lesson going wrong. An expert teacher typically heads off the prospective crash before it happens, by having an acute and subtle sense of how in tune students are with the learning.

Having experienced many, many failures, I can attest to having a hardened sense of crisis management!

Expert teachers can anticipate issues. Attempting to teach some beautiful poetry by Percy Shelley or a rip-roaring Jacobean tragedy requires a thorough working knowledge of the barriers students

Dealing with observations

face. 'We can't understand it Sir!' 'Why do we have to read this? We already do history Miss.' Most English teachers have had the Shakespeare debate, the poetry debate, the answers-are-on-Google debate.

They have conquered the supposed hatred of poetry by unveiling a love of lyrics and discussing emotion and language that mean something to students. They know that the teaching of the semicolon appears to be couched in mystery, judging by the continued misuse of this special little punctuation mark.

These knowledgeable teachers see off these issues at the pass. They make Shakespeare relevant before they introduce Shakespeare. They relate the best of poetry to the best of music. They unveil the dark mysteries of punctuation and show why it is important to meaning and to their future.

Seek out that expert knowledge all around you. Often, the greatest teachers will be humble and unassuming about their talents, but they'll be more than happy to share. Reflect on when your lessons went wrong and diagnose what you can do better. Share your reflections with the very same humble, expert teachers in your department.

Don't be afraid to deviate from the plan, or even scrap it all together. If a group is not willing to undertake group work sensibly, then you might have to change course and have the students work individually. If they simply don't understand why to use discourse markers in their argument writing, then it may require a hastily rejigged lesson plan to focus upon that writing skill.

You can attempt to head off these issues by planning for some alternative approaches, if there are issues with student understanding. Usually, these issues aren't predictable and are pretty much spontaneous. If you factor in a 'hinge-point' task or question to diagnose knowledge and understanding, you can often manage where you want students to go in the lesson.

A reality is that some classes you teach would not be your selection for an observation. An *interesting* class, euphemistically put, often requires the most planning and forethought to avoid the lesson crashing. The simple principle stands for all classes, but most definitely the *'interesting'* classes: stick to your core routines, exercise infinite patience and train students relentlessly to have good working habits. This will reduce the likelihood of the lesson disappearing off piste.

Listen to, and act upon, your observation feedback

It may not feel like it at times, but, as a new teacher, you have the privilege of lots of feedback from observations that help shape your practice. Even expert teachers can plateau, owing to their lack of constructive feedback to help hone what they do once they have passed their early years in teaching.

Take every opportunity to get feedback on your English teaching.

When it doesn't go well, it can be hard to listen dispassionately to criticisms, no matter how constructive they may be. What we must do is conquer the emotion of the observation experience, moving past disappointment or delight, to better apply what we have learned to our future practice.

Good lesson feedback will often be in the form of questions such as, 'What was the point where student behaviour dipped and why?', or 'Which students struggled with the writing task and why?'. Open 'why' questions cleverly prompt your own self-reflection, helping you find the answers yourself. Sometimes, a simple but precise observation, such as encouraging you to increase wait times when asking questions, can be tiny in terms of time and effort, but significant in terms of impact. It is important to mentally bank these gems of advice.

You may keep a *reflective journal*, make notes or write a blog about your teaching. Whatever you do, it is crucial to reflect. Being a reflective practitioner sounds like educational jargon, but it is some of the most important advice you will receive.

The job of being an English teacher is terrifically complex (which brings with it the rich, varied experience that we sought when we applied to teach English), and, therefore, we need to break it down into its component parts. By taking each piece of feedback and applying it systematically to our subsequent lessons, we make crucial marginal gains towards becoming a great English teacher.

All teachers have their strengths and their areas to improve. We would be inhuman if this were not the case. We should listen sensitively to our feedback and aim to build a coherent pattern of our professional skills. We should then commit ourselves to getting better.

In great schools, we will get ample support to do this, but this will not always be the case. Sometimes, our improvement will have to be a process that is driven by us and our intrinsic motivation to be a great English teacher.

ACTIVITY

You are going to be observed in a couple of weeks, with your most challenging class. They can prove difficult in terms of behaviour and they want their lessons to follow the path of least resistance, otherwise they can play up. It isn't a scenario that is too difficult to visualise for a novice teacher.

- What preparatory steps do you take, beyond teaching great lessons as consistently as possible? Who do you speak to for advice about the group?
- What learning habits do you most want your students to exhibit, and how will your lesson plan aid your pursuit?
- What behaviour management mechanisms do you have in place in case of 'emergency'?
- What would you say in conversation with your observer the week before?
- If it goes worse than you imagined, what are your next steps to ensure teaching and learning for this group improve?

CASE STUDY: WHEN YOU JUST DON'T KNOW

My initial teacher training was quite different to that of my colleagues, in that I learned 'on the job', through the now-obsolete Graduate Teacher Programme. Over the course of the GTP, I was observed twenty times. Before my first lesson (and observation), I remember thinking, 'But I don't know *how*!'

That lesson was graded 'Satisfactory with Good features', in old Ofsted parlance, and, although I could hardly have expected an 'Outstanding' on my first attempt, I have to admit I was disappointed.

This leads me to my first piece of advice: don't take criticism personally. I still find it hard not to get emotional during observation feedback – teaching *is* personal – but I have become much better at not beating myself up so much for what I perceive 'went wrong'. A good observer will give you constructive criticism, and you will become better at hearing it.

The temptation with an observed lesson is to 'go down with the ship' and stick to the plan, but if, for whatever reason, it isn't working, you must adapt your lesson. One of my 'Outstanding' lessons at times bore no relation to the lesson plan I had written! Your observer will give you credit, and, more importantly, you will know for next time what the class can or cannot manage.

Initial teacher training is an intense experience, and the observations may feel relentless, but my final word of advice is to try to embrace the challenge. Stressful though they are, observations are really just opportunities to continue to develop your pedagogy. Show that you can act on feedback and showcase what you are truly capable of achieving.

Nicole Fletcher, English Teacher

CASE STUDY: LESSON OBSERVATIONS FROM A HEAD-TEACHER-AS-OBSERVER'S PERSPECTIVE

Ask any set of students for the five key features of a good teacher, and they will give you essentially the same answer: good teachers are enthusiastic; they make lessons fun; they know their subject; they respect us as adults; they help if we don't understand. Ask a student – I bet you find I'm right! Observations are all about seeing things from the students' perspective.

You need to explain to the teacher that you really don't mind if s/he does not follow the lesson plan; explain how you won't be focusing upon their teaching – what you are bothered about is whether the students are engaged in learning.

Ban timings on lesson plans; over-planned lessons are a curse. And then, when the lesson begins, just gauge how interested the students feel. Talk to them. Look in their books – do the students have pride in what they are doing? See how *you* feel and whether *you* are engaged in what is being taught. Look out for moments when the lesson moves on and judge whether the students are ready or whether they need to spend more time on that particular element of their learning first; hinge-point stuff – *how sensitive is the teacher's assessment radar?*

I'm also interested in opportunities for the lesson to move in an unplanned direction due to a student's fascinating, off-the-wall question; I've seen student enthusiasm systematically crushed in the worst lessons and blossom gloriously in the best. I want to be dazzled in lessons. I don't want tricks, or a series of pacy activities; I don't mind if the students do one thing all lesson, as long as they are on task and engaged.

I want to see students enjoying what they're doing and learning; *it's that simple and that complex.*

John Tomsett, Head Teacher and English Teacher

TALKING POINTS

- Do you know what your strengths and weaknesses are? How are you developing and improving upon your strengths?
- What good habits of pedagogy have you established that clearly exhibit the students are making excellent progress to your observer?
- How do you respond to feedback? Do you need to think or act differently when responding to lesson feedback?

Note

1   This can be found on the Ofsted website: 'English Subject Specific Guidance for Inspectors Making Judgement'; see www.ofsted.gov.uk/ resources/generic-grade-descriptors-and-supplementary-subject-specific-guidance-for-inspectors-making-judgement

9 Dealing with pressure

Being an English teacher is undoubtedly one of the more high-pressured jobs in secondary school teaching. Literacy and English teaching will always be central to judgements made by governments when determining the success of secondary school students. English will always be crucial to school leaders, parents and the students themselves.

But you knew that already.

Embrace the challenge and the overt recognition that teaching English matters. The hundreds of relationships you form with children, the books you select to read and the legions of daily decisions that you make in your role matter.

You can make a positive difference to the lives of children. This may appear trite or grandiose to some, but it is true. In whatever small way, it is true.

When the pressure builds, with any and all aspects of the job, just remember why you are doing it and why the job matters. It will make the pressures feel like they are worth it.

What we must do is aim to manage these pressures and manage ourselves. I am not advocating short cuts or the abrogation of our responsibility, but, instead, that you are pragmatic. You need to organise, prioritise and balance your workload.

Novice teachers will inevitably take longer to complete the most basic of tasks, from marking to lesson planning and the range of administrative tasks required daily. Teachers are often mis-represented in the tabloid newspapers regarding how many holi-days they have, etc. The reality is a gruelling treadmill of multiple daily 'performances' in the classroom, rewarded by holidays where you receive the gift of essay marking, lesson planning and body-deadening tiredness!

Most teachers will articulate to you the difficulties of achiev-ing a work–life balance. This is indeed a concern. This chapter will hopefully help you mitigate some of the issues you will face and give you workable tips to manage the challenge of teaching English.

Achieving the balance is difficult, but it is achievable.

One important aspect of dealing with pressure is ensuring that you have support. Make sure that you take every opportunity in your professional development to improve and get support. If observing other excellent teachers will help you develop your practice, then seek out such experiences relentlessly.

If there are books/resources/courses that you think can help you develop your practice, then don't be afraid to ask. In fact, the key is having the confidence to ask.

Don't bottle up your fears and anxieties. Seek out support and ask as many questions as you can. The best new teachers are the teachers who ask the most questions of other teachers and their leaders.

'Keep the main thing the main thing': the planning and marking rule

Being an English teacher can be a highly creative job. You get the privileged opportunity to make literature a part of your working life. The job is varied and rich with unique people and experiences. This is coupled with the less creative challenges of report planning or essay marking. A great English teacher has to be committed, but crucially they must be well organised.

Dealing with pressure

The novice teacher may take twice as long as an experienced teacher to complete the very same tasks. You'll be given some more non-teaching time to cope with these demands, but such time will always feel rather inadequate relative to the work that you need to do.

Given the limitations of being a novice, it is important to prioritise the tasks that require our precious time.

Lesson planning and marking are the two towering tasks to which we should devote the vast bulk of our time. As indicated in the assessment chapter (**Chapter 4**), it is important to undertake purposeful peer- and self-assessment to help manage your marking workload.

Invest your time early in the school year in training your students for such purposeful AfL. Second, make sure your marking and feedback are targeted. You will not retain a semblance of a life if you attempt to mark everything a student has written. Not only that, they would become wholly dependent on your feedback if this were the case. Get yourself a marking rota. Create your own personal deadlines and compare them with deadlines for other tasks, such as school reports, etc.

Lesson planning can be annoyingly slow when you do not have the expert access to a host of strategies rooted in a deep reservoir of prior knowledge. Get as much help from your colleagues as possible – many of your fellow English teachers will have been there and done that – and, therefore, they'll possess some resources that will save you valuable time.

Another crucial piece of advice is not to devote an excessive amount of time to creating or recreating resources that will have a finite use. Creating laminated character cards, for example, may be time consuming and actually inferior to simply getting students to sketch quickly on paper.

The '**Pareto principle**'[1] summarises neatly how you need to dedicate your time to be an effective English teacher – otherwise known as 'the law of the valuable few'. Identify what small number of factors has the most impact upon your teaching and learning.

For example, the impact of *feedback* on student progress is incontrovertible; therefore, marking with good formative feedback should be at the core of your 'valuable few'. Lesson planning gives you a crucial opportunity to develop your learning patterns and the good habits that you need students to follow. The more experienced you become, the less dependent you are upon lesson plans, but early on they are reliable ballast in your teaching hold.

Another common area in which to invest your time in the early days is behaviour management. This time can be spent in various ways. Committing yourself to following through on misbehaviour is a non-negotiable use of your time if you want to become a great teacher. If you follow up relentlessly, when a student misses their homework for example, they will think twice before doing so again.

Taking time to observe how other teachers manage behaviour, or reading one of the many useful books or blog posts on behaviour management, will be an investment that ultimately saves you a great deal of time and energy down the road.

Actively manage your time

I was never much of an organised list maker before I became an English teacher. In fact, I wasn't very organised at all. As a new teacher, I was quickly shocked into action. It started with scraps of notes, but I soon became an organised list maker. I had to, and you likely will too.

Make lists – in a notebook, on your smart phone or on your tablet device. Whatever you do, organise the sheer complexity of the job and prioritise your tasks.

An important part of prioritising your to-do list is to allocate the required time and deadline to your list. This adds greater clarity and allows you to make clear *when* and *where* you *need* to complete your jobs. Here is my simple example to-do list (rather optimistically short!):

Dealing with pressure

1   **Priority 1** – Marking Year 10 homework (*4 hours – at home – tonight!*).

2   **Priority 2** – Plan *A Christmas Carol* for Year 8 scheme of learning (*3 hours – in lunchtime detentions – by next Friday – 24th*).

3   **Priority 3** – See subject leader re: English literature moderation (15 minutes – by the end of the week).

Many people divide their priorities in terms of *daily, weekly* and *termly* targets. This is an eminently sensible approach. You will find certain school terms a challenge.

Those glossy adverts for new teachers don't represent the reality of energy-sapping winter colds, propped up only by some Lemsips and a monumental pile of marking midway through December! Christmas soon heralds the season of recuperation and haggard goodwill.

ACTIVITY

It is coming to the end of November, and you have a couple of weeks to ensure students in three of your groups have completed their summative assessments and have had all their work marked. You also have a school open evening. Not only that, you have been asked to help with the school pantomime (you love pantomimes!), and you have a family weekend planned.

- What decisions do you need to make in terms of prioritisation?
- How would you list the jobs in terms of priority, and would you say no to any of the above?
- How do you ensure some semblance of a work–life balance to keep you sane?

Learn the power of 'no'

In the brave new dawn of a new post in a new school, you will rightly want to plunge yourself deeply into the life of the school. It is important to involve yourself in the school community and develop a positive presence and reputation for yourself. But getting the right *balance* is the thing.

A wise man once told me he used the phrase, 'I'll get back to you on that one', as a sure-fire way of saying no in the politest terms! Refer to your brilliantly organised calendar and to-do lists and make an informed choice about saying 'yes' to any invitations, however appetising!

There are peaks and troughs throughout the school year in terms of workload. Seek out advice about balancing your year ahead. Holidays for English teachers, particularly new teachers, are rather a false dawn. Planning your marking demands you use some of your holiday time – sometimes significantly so. Again, marking and planning are the two pillars of your practice. That being said, do allocate yourself time for some good rest, particularly during the longer Easter and Summer holidays.

Actively build a support network, within and without school

The challenging experiences of new recruits into the teaching profession are, in many ways, individual and wholly unique to you; however, many experienced teachers have gone through much the same difficulties and stresses that you will be going through and will be more than happy to help. Some will gleefully share their war stories, which sometimes hinder more than they help!

Just remember, people can be inclined to moan at work, so just keep an open mind about your progress and your students'.

 As already stated, don't suffer in silence. **Twitter**, blogs, **TES forums** and legions of websites connect to a wider world of education beyond your school. Some trainees have the misfortune

171

of not having a natural and positive support network in school, but fear not: you can now develop personal networks outside school.

You can attend **TeachMeets,** or be part of professional networks, such as the TES, which have helpful forums on hot topics such as behaviour management. Often, simply knowing that many fellow struggling teachers are facing similar challenges to you is enough to boost your confidence.

You will be assigned a mentor, who you should meet regularly and who can guide you through choppy waters. You will have fellow new starters, or NQTs, at your school. Most schools have coordinated programmes for you to share your development and to find support. If your school does not do this well, then aim to foster relationships with fellow new teachers and build the network you need yourself.

Each new teacher has different relationship and family circumstances. Most people do not have partners or parents who understand life teaching in a school. If you do, then you are lucky. If you don't, then be prepared to have the difficulties and growing pains of teaching impinge on your personal life.

Do *make* family time and have time with friends. It can be the most crucial release valve from all your pressures. If you have to timetable your family life and your personal pleasures, then do so.

Don't let your career consume your life. Aim to work at maintaining your relationships. As important as teaching undoubtedly is, it is not worth irreparably damaging your most important relationships.

The wise philosopher Alain de Botton said: 'There is no such thing as work–life balance. Everything worth fighting for unbalances your life.' English teachers will find a great deal of truth in that aphorism.

Ride the roller coaster of emotion

The metaphor of a roller coaster may appear rather hackneyed, but I cannot think of a more accurate description of the job of a new English teacher. So much so, I use it regularly. On some days, you will think you are cheating by having a job where you get to discuss your passion and knowledge of the world of words with willing participants. On other days, you will regret you ever heard the name of Bill Shakespeare!

Each new experience – parents' evening, school trips to the theatre, etc. – will all bring a palpable sense of anxiety and excitement. Tiredness and illness may well beset your early attempts at teaching excellence. Aim to even out your highs and lows and consciously pace your year ahead. Keep one eye on your calendar and another on your marking and planning materials.

It is important to keep things in perspective. You *will* have lessons, often planned with immaculate precision, that fail. Some failures will be spectacular. There may be tears before break time.

In my NQT year, I remember vividly teaching what was a very nice and a very able Year 11 English group. We were studying poetry in a mouldering hut of a classroom. It was a wet and steamy Wednesday afternoon. For whatever reason, or combination of reasons, they were completely unwilling to focus . . . or listen . . . or behave. The small-scale misbehaviours kept on coming: talking while I was talking, kicking chairs – a real death by a thousand cuts. My tiredness and tension got the better of me. I simply stopped teaching them. I allowed them either to work on the task I had set or to talk for the last twenty minutes.

One student, sitting in front of me, took the opportunity to do the work and not simply talk away the time. That one girl gave me the impetus to come back strong. After an early night, the following day I had the group before lunchtime. I acted like nothing had happened. Then, at the end of the lesson, I kept the entire class in to work for half an hour, making up the work they had missed the day before.

All except for the girl who had chosen to work.

I spoke to them all at the end of the lunchtime detention. I confidently reasserted my authority. I warned them that I would not let them fail, and that I expected an equal commitment from them.

That day was a turning point. I had questioned whether I was able to become a good teacher. By the end of the next day, I knew that I could.

You will, no doubt, have similar experiences. One of the essential qualities that the best English teachers have is a relentless sense of determination and willingness to persevere. A toughness. With a commitment to improve, any natural dips or plateaus in your teaching can be overcome. It just takes some skill and no little amount of *grit*.

Possess a 'growth mindset'

Carol Dweck, in her excellent book on behavioural psychology, *Mindset: How You Can Fulfil Your Potential*, defined two potential mindsets: a *'fixed mindset'* and a *'growth mindset'*. A fixed mindset applies to those people, both students and teachers, who have a fixed idea that talent is set, who perceive feedback as criticism and who are averse to taking on challenges for fear of failing. In contrast, a growth mindset applies to people who see talent as something defined by effort, who have a willingness to learn and fail, or even look silly, if it means they get better.

For some teachers, such psychological traits are to be attributed solely to our students, but we ourselves are exempt. Instead, we should face our own learning with such honesty. Many English teachers have experienced a lifetime of success, from being a fluent reader at school to writing exemplary essays at university. When faced with a reluctant group of Year 10 students, such expertise can actually inhibit our success.

The *'curse of the expert'* is the potential for us to be unable to remember, or even understand, the difficulties faced by students. Not only that, failing to teach successfully, something that happens weekly or daily as a new teacher, threatens our sense of self and our confidence in our expertise.

Try reading a book in a foreign language, one you have vague memories of from your schooldays. The lack of fluency you experience is dispiriting. It feels awkward and far from enjoyable. It can feel like failure. This is the experience of many of our students on a daily basis. It is hard for our students to have a 'growth mindset', or a willingness to learn, in these circumstances. We must help foster that resilience and grit in our students. We can start by modelling it in our own practice.

Almost all teachers will go through struggles that challenge our sense of self. These experiences will build pressure and prick our anxieties. We need to face them with equanimity.

CASE STUDY: UNDER PRESSURE

It will hit you and it will hit you hard!

You just can't escape the fact that, when you embrace the world of teaching, you'll end up being completely drained by Christmas! Yes, you'll wonder why you did it, and at times you'll wonder where the exit door is. However, you can survive!

For me, the most important thing is perspective. What we do is so important but crucially, it isn't a matter of life and death. When you're up against it you need to turn to your colleagues around you – there's no need to try to pretend you're the Herculean figure who has all the answers – we've all been there.

It's crucial that you take a step back and realise that the most important thing for your students is your ability to deliver 'good lessons'. Make 'good enough' be your mantra. It's not possible to deliver 'outstanding' every day, even though 'outstanding' may be our ultimate goal.

Organisation is essential – your time both in and out of school.

You'll have a slightly lighter timetable at first – use it!

Dealing with pressure

Speak to those around you and borrow from their systems –
for marking, lesson planning, report writing – even the things
you didn't even know needed to be done!

Outside of school you will see your own time sucked away
from you. Yes, it does suck!

This is why you *have to* have some allotted 'me time'.
Whatever it might be: the cinema, gym or origami. If you don't
find time for 'you', you'll resent the job and perhaps wonder
why you do it. Don't feel guilty about leaving school at a
sensible time and having a life!

You work incredibly hard – you deserve, and need, that time
to step back, reflect and work out that yes, you do enjoy it after
all!

**Karl Elwell, Subject Leader of Media
and English Teacher**

CASE STUDY: NQT PRESSURE

In my NQT year there were plenty of new pressures to deal
with: deadlines, marking and lesson observations. Of these, I
found working to a deadline the most challenging. I was
working in a large and busy department, where my colleagues
appeared to be cool, calm and collected – which can easily
make you feel cut adrift in a sea of unknowns.

After getting over my hesitations about appearing the
uninitiated 'newbie', I began asking questions and discovered
that not only were the other members of my department happy
to answer my questions, but many were thankful of the
opportunity to voice their own confusion.

Marking was a close second in my pressure calendar. The
dual responsibility of being an accurate marker and utilising
vague and new criteria led to some rather obscure initial
annotations on my students' papers. My saving grace was

asking my colleagues to cast their eye over any borderline pieces, and actually accepting that when it comes to annotation, there isn't a magic formula that you can adopt.

Just trust your gut instinct and seek out support if required.

In my second week I was catapulted into the teaching arena with a double KS5 lesson teaching the poetical wonders of Auden, observed by my subject leader (and mentor) and the head teacher! I coped with the stresses of being observed by keeping it in perspective. It wasn't perfect, but I knew I would learn from my mistakes.

Ultimately, the best advice I could give to an NQT would be to be organised, to not be afraid to ask questions (even if they seem silly!) and to let go of the pressure to be perfect. It's important to acknowledge that as an NQT you are not the finished article. That's the beauty of learning – the only way is up!

Heather Maycock, English Teacher

TALKING POINTS

- Are you an organised person? Be honest! What do you need to do to better organise your professional and personal life?
- What is your mindset when approaching your working life? How will you better deal with setbacks? Who is your support network, particularly when you need help to deal with setbacks?

Note

1   This can be found on the Internet; see http://en.wikipedia.org/wiki/Pareto_principle

10 Applying for your first English teacher post

Teaching is a demanding, difficult and simultaneously deeply enriching vocation. Unfortunately, too many teachers leave the profession early and never persevere to experience the brilliant rewards of seeing students succeed and making a tangible difference to the lives of young people.

It is, therefore, paramount that you make a well-informed judgement about schools where you apply for an English job. I'm sure that the vast bulk of those who entered the profession and left relatively quickly had their experience determined by the limitations of one school, or even one English department. Some schools simply do a far better job of guiding you through the particularly challenging early years.

It may sound like a trite cliché, but it is crucial to find the right school for you.

There is what appears to be a dizzying array of school types, with varying cohorts of students, different curriculum models, different support networks, and so on. The sheer breadth of schools alone can be daunting. For a decision that is clearly so crucial, ample research is essential. Some decisions in life cannot be predicted, but we can make a sound case for having as much evidence as possible to shape our decision-making.

Sometimes, trainee teachers are lucky enough to land a plum job at the school in which they trained, where they have intimate knowledge of the staff and school systems. Of course, many more have to undertake the search for a job in a highly competitive field, without all the answers. It is, therefore, crucial to develop a support network, including professional contacts, that can help steer you and provide some reliable expert knowledge. As you would expect, there are a wealth of support resources on the Internet that can help steer your professional ship.

Entry into the teaching profession seems to change ceaselessly. We appear to be experiencing a momentous shift from conventional **PGCE** (Postgraduate Certificate of Education) courses undertaken at university, with school placements, to a school-led system, with students training at **teaching schools**, often with links to the local university. Add to that other organisations and pathways, such as **Teach First**, **GTP** (Graduate Teacher Programme), **Schools Direct** and **S-CITT** (School-Centred Initial Teacher Training), and you could be forgiven for being confused.

Here are some useful websites to start making sense of the myriad of options:

- www.education.gov.uk/get-into-teaching: a useful one-stop shop for guidance on entering the profession, particularly for the **S-CITT** and **GTP** routes;

- http://graduates.teachfirst.org.uk: this website gives you all the information you need about this specific route into teaching.

Develop a network of contacts

Many new teachers have been inspired to teach by those great teachers who touch our hearts and inspire within us a life-long love of literature and English learning. Some people are lucky enough to still be in contact with such people; others no doubt have friends or family who can give them some useful advice regarding the teaching application process. Undeniably, a new or prospective English teacher needs to quickly establish a supportive network of people who know the ropes.

Applying for your first English teacher post

Most trainee English teachers will first encounter **S-CITT**, **PGCE** or **GTP** course leaders or mentors. Such people are trained to help you develop your working knowledge of job applications, etc. With **Teach First**, once you have met its criteria and have been accepted on to its course, you will be allocated a teaching role in a school selected for you.

Beyond these crucial figures in your training, it pays to spread your net as wide as possible. This may include some of the following strategies to develop your network of supportive contacts:

- Attend local ITT courses or conferences.

- Attend **TeachMeets** (a less formal sharing of best practice between teachers – *free*, and you can even choose to take part; see www.teachmeet.pbworks.com).

- Build a **PLN** (professional learning network) on social media websites such as **Twitter**. You can find authors, writers of teacher training tomes and an army of English teachers who are happily sharing ideas and resources. Weekly chats are undertaken, such as **#ukedchat** and **#engchatuk**, that provide a nexus for like-minded teachers.

- Join and trawl online networks, such as http://community.tes.co.uk or www.guardian.co.uk/teacher-network, for useful articles, comment sections and chat facilities.

- Make contact with educational bloggers on popular platforms such as **WordPress** or **Blogger**.

- Make connections through your teaching union, or seek out links with local school networks. If you are in a teaching school, you will be linked to a local learning network. Most academy schools are part of a chain of schools that actively collaborate and share resources, approach and guidance.

The process can be time consuming and sometimes frustrating, but building a network of professional contacts can be invaluable in giving you insights and helping you find the right job for you.

Researching the right school and role for you

Many factors, such as geographical factors, have a crucial impact upon your choice of school. Our own experiences of school often colour our professional choices. Other factors, based on political or ideological affiliation, may sway you in one way or another.

Here is a list of factors you may wish to consider in your decision-making process:

- **11–16 or 11–18 school?** Some teachers view teaching KS5 students as crucial to their decision. Others prefer working with younger students. Experience of both is useful and desirable. This can obviously affect the scope of your teaching and the diversity of your experience.

- **Single sex or mixed gender?** A quite personal consideration, but with some practical considerations for teaching and learning.

- **School type?** *Academy, LEA maintained school, faith schools, comprehensive schools, free schools, grammar schools* or the *independent* sector – the list is long ... and growing! The contextual factors that relate to each school make this area an essential factor in choosing the right school for you. Political viewpoint, contractual implications, student intake, school culture, etc., all require careful consideration. Although school structures are subject to near constant change, it is important to take individual schools on their own merits.

- **Selective or comprehensive school intake?** As above, the structure of the school is key. The school intake has significant implications for your teaching position. Many teachers would see working in a selective school as being an 'easier' option, but selective schools have their own pressures, be it results or additional expectations of teachers.

- **Distance:** Being an English teacher is always something I would recommend, but I would never label it easy! Practical considerations such as the proximity of the school to your home are really important. After a long day of teaching, any significant amount of time stuck in traffic or on public transport is bound to test the nerves.

- **'Reputation, reputation, reputation'**: Shakespeare was rarely wrong! The reputation of a school is crucial. Rarely is it far wrong, and it can become a self-fulfilling prophecy, as a school with an outstanding reputation invariably attracts lots of students and supportive parents, which typically has a positive impact upon outcomes at the other end.

- **Pay and conditions**: The teaching profession is new to the variables of *performance-related pay* and flexibility in pay arrangements. It does mean each and every school is free to set its own contracts and differentiate by pay and conditions. The salary figures will, of course, be important information, but just as important could be the contractual small print. Many schools will provide better conditions, support and protections for new members of staff. Research with care!

Know where to find the right jobs as soon as they become available

Just as pathways into teaching are changing ceaselessly, finding the most appropriate place to source your first post is undergoing change. If you are pursuing the **Teach First** route, then your choice will be made for you.

All other pathways typically follow a standard route of people independently searching for teaching posts. Many trainees are fortunate enough to find that their placement school has offered them a job. The vast majority undertakes the search everywhere.

Most jobs are advertised in the summer term, but you really should start looking at the turn of the year.

Here is a useful list of the primary sources of English teacher advertisements:

- **TES Jobs**: *The Times Educational Supplement* is produced in newspaper and electronic form. The website can provide you with useful alerts for jobs that fit your specified criteria. This is a very popular route for schools to take. TES provides a section exclusively for NQTs.

- *The Guardian* has its own job section that covers education and teaching.

- **Eteach.com**: This private website provides an easy-to-navigate website of teacher jobs. You can enter 'job pools' through eteach.com, which circulate your details to local schools or regional talent pools.

- **Teaching pools**: Many regions and local education authorities run 'teaching pools'. This means that, in the autumn, you create your curriculum vitae and profile and you automatically place yourself as available for jobs that fit your criteria in that 'teaching pool'.

- **School and academy websites**: Increasingly, schools are advertising their jobs locally. Internal vacancy bulletins from local councils, academy vacancy pages and school website vacancy sections are all now used to advertise jobs or to supplement national advertisements. Adding some of these websites to your *favourites* may well prove a wise move, so you don't miss out.

The following national websites are useful for advice:

- Department of Education: www.education.gov.uk/schools
- Training and Development Agency for Schools: www.tda.co.uk
- Advice for NQTs and links to job pages: www.teachernet.gov.uk
- Links to all county councils' web pages: www.direct.gov.uk

Research the specific school you wish to apply for in as much depth as possible

A job advertisement only ever tells part of the story. You need to go the extra mile and research every aspect of the school possible. Any successful application is rooted in a sound knowledge of the school and the specific English job advertised. You need to personalise your application and work out whether the school suits you and your needs as a new teacher.

Consider researching the following:

- **School website**: This is a goldmine of information if you are seeking the inside track on a school. Websites vary in quality, but you will notice a pattern for each school website that can unveil important truths about any school. First, does the school have a core purpose and a values system that are explicit on its website? Do the news and events show the school lives those values? Does the English department emerge vibrantly through the website, or is it a token footnote in a link? What other aspects of the school are prominent – for example, school trips, local news or special events?

- **School newsletter(s)**: Many schools now have website links to their school newsletter (targeted at parents). Can you glean any useful nuggets from there?

- **Exam results data**: School league tables and school websites publish exam results very publicly. Of course, English results feature very prominently. Do these results give you an indication of the challenges ahead? Are sky-high results the norm, or does the English department need to make significant improvements? Do be aware that exam results are often a self-fulfilling prophecy. If a school is selective by ability, its results are almost guaranteed to be high. It may not accurately reflect the strengths or weaknesses of the English department. An English department is not always the sum of its examination results, in lots of ways!

• **Ofsted reports**: These reports are uniquely couched in jargon, but they can be a blunt tool for taking the temperature of a school. Don't be sold by an 'Outstanding' judgement and don't be put off by a 'Requiring improvement'. Appearances can be deceiving. The new Ofsted dashboard facility (http://dashboard. ofsted.gov.uk) gives you progress data for English that can give you useful information well worthy of raising at interview or in your letter of application.

• **Request a school visit**: If at all possible, visit the school and get a real sense of the inner workings of the place. Often, the head teacher will willingly give you a tour of the school. This can be illuminating, while giving you an opportunity to leave a very positive impression.

• **Mine your contacts**: Teaching is a small world. Attempt to scour your professional contacts to squeeze out any useful information about a school.

ACTIVITY

You have trained in a direct placement at a single-sex academy and you have never felt like you have been given the requisite support needed to be a success. You have been given repeated judgements of 'requiring improvement', but you believe that you are a good teacher. You begin looking for a new school.

• What are your primary considerations for selecting a school that is right for you?
• Where do you seek the best advice for your next career steps?
• How do you inform your prospective school, in a professional manner, that you haven't enjoyed your training experience?

Read your application pack with great care, and prepare to personalise your application

Once you have committed to requesting the application pack from a given school, it is time to apply your expert reading skills! Often, the information in the pack can be sourced from the school website, but do pay particular attention to the department-specific information that will be useful for your letter of application.

Have a highlighter to hand and skim the pack for the general gist. How is the school represented in the pack? What is the English department like from appearances, e.g. size, scope of curriculum, etc.? What are the specifics of the role? What are the crucial points of information you need to digest? What do you need to know?

Start scanning for the essential nuggets of information that you want to include in your application. Is the English department *'passionate about reading'*? Does the school have a 'whole-school literacy drive' relevant to the post? Does the role include 'a range of KS5 teaching'? etc. Scan to find and define the core strengths of the school and the English department. *Where do you and your skills fit into that picture?*

Aim to make notes that synthesise your reading and make a specific note of important questions that you need answering. Some questions, such as pay and conditions, may well be answerable with a quick phone call, whereas others may require an interview to unpick answers.

If you are working and making multiple applications, this process will feel gruelling, but the effort does pay off. Better to maximise your efforts and not miss out on an interview for a dream job than forever be kicking yourself that you didn't apply.

Write an accurate and brilliant application

Let's get this right. You are applying for a job as an English teacher. You must be accurate with your punctuation, spelling and grammar. No other job has the inalienable right to select one similar candidate over another, based on the correct use of the semicolon! Write your letter and proofread it multiple times.

Ask a reliable reading friend to read it for accuracy – ideally one of those friends who exhibit pedantry about grammar, hitherto never so crucial and useful.

Crucially, your application needs to follow these simple rules:

1   **It should be personalised to the school.** A generic, brief letter too easily smacks of a lack of effort on the part of the applicant. You should exhibit a good knowledge of the school, based on the application pack and your wider knowledge. It may look something like this:

> _____ School has a clear ethos to help its students become confident and successful learners, with continual focus on challenging each individual to reach their full potential. This sense of potential, coupled with the high standards and the highest expectations of its students and staff, makes _____ School a thriving institution, and I would relish the opportunity to become a part of this supportive school.

2   **It should address the 'person specification'.** Each English teacher job will follow a typical 'person specification' that lists the skills, experience and qualifications required for the job. These include points such as: 'excellent subject knowledge in English language and literature', 'able to work successfully as part of a team', 'willingness to contribute to the wider life of the school', etc. Here is an example of how you could answer the specification regarding _'working successfully as part of a team'_:

> I have a great belief in the importance of collaborative learning for both students and staff. I have developed my

187

skills in a highly supportive department at my training school and I have found the sharing of ideas and experience an invaluable resource. I recently worked with my colleagues in devising new and innovative schemes of learning for the teaching of Shakespeare at KS3. Independently, I shared a scheme I developed personally for English language A level, focusing upon exam revision. I would like to contribute my own energy and creativity to the vibrant and committed English Department at _____ School and become a conscientious part of the team.

3 **It should relate your experience relevant to the post.** You may not be able to exemplify every aspect of the post. For example, you may not have taught KS5 extensively, but you may have some experience of teaching or supporting KS5, and your degree will, of course, exhibit your subject knowledge. You might include a paragraph that looks something like this:

My degree at the University of Liverpool encompassed both English literature and English language. The breadth of my degree gives me a broad overview of English, as well as the confidence to teach these at the highest level. I would be confident in teaching KS5 students in both A level subjects. In my training school I team-taught and supported an English literature group throughout the school year. I greatly enjoyed the dynamic interactions between the students and I learned a great deal about differentiating between students at that level. I believe I am equipped with the subject knowledge to quickly develop my skills at this key stage.

4 **It should convey your passion for English and teaching children.** This is your sole opportunity to relate your commitment to teaching students and teaching English. It is a privilege and a challenge. You need to leave the reader in no doubt about your passion and energy. There is a strong likelihood that the ethos

of the school chimes with your passion. This may look something like this model paragraph:

> I am unequivocally passionate about teaching English and passing on the rich wealth of literature at the heart of our culture. The study of language and literature is crucial in helping students both understand the world around them and communicate with confidence so they can thrive at _____ School and beyond.

5   **It must be clearly structured.** There is no exact formula or paragraph plan, but you may want to consider the following list as a guideline:

- Have an opening paragraph stating your interest in the post.

- Second, state why you are applying to that particular school and why you match its requirements.

- Beyond that, you should clearly outline your relevant experience and qualities that match the person specification.

- You may be asked to state your philosophy of education. Mark yourself out as a candidate who is up to date with the debates surrounding education.

- Finally, convey your personal interests and wider experiences. Sometimes, beyond the jargon of meeting the 'person specification', you can mark your application out by revealing your human qualities. Those small personal details may well be the factor that helps you get that interview.

6   **It must be accurate.** Get someone to proofread your efforts. Many an English application has fallen at this particular hurdle. Your style and sentence structures shouldn't be overcomplicated. Your spelling, punctuation and grammar should be flawless.

ACTIVITY

Undertake some 'blue-sky thinking'. Describe your perfect school. Consider all the aspects that make it the ideal school for you. Write an impassioned letter of application for this school.

This task provides you with multiple benefits. Hopefully, it will furnish you with an excellent covering letter draft that is ripe for adaptation. It will make you consider what type of school you need to teach in and ensure you keep the bar high in your selection. It may also provide you with a future goal. Perhaps that school needs creating, and you can help do it.

CASE STUDY: BE YOURSELF

Securing your first job can be an arduous task. As with any potential job application, you must find an employer that is suitable for you. A post at one school might be perfect for Adam Lewis, but could equally be disastrous for Alex Quigley. When searching for a school, ensure the following:

- You know what kind of training you'll be getting. There seems to be a shift from GTP and PGCE training to Schools Direct and Teach First. Ensure you're applying for the right course for you and your needs.
- You research the school. As well as you knowing what you're getting yourself into, it impresses the school if you know something about it.
- Be completely honest in your application. Your potential employers will be able to pick out any holes in your application if you're telling porky pies. Equally, don't undersell yourself.

Once you get the interview, there are certain things you can do to help with nerves. Make sure that:

- You have practised potential questions. Although you cannot predict every question they will ask you at interview, you can guess some of the topics that will be covered. If possible, get someone who has taken part in the interviewing process to give you feedback on your answers.
- Read through your application form so that you know what the school is likely to ask. They are not there to catch you out, but want you to showcase your strengths.

Finally, on interview day, make sure that you are yourself. You do not want to pretend to be something you're not; otherwise, when you actually start working at the school, both you and the school might be in for a nasty shock. It's going to end in tears if they're expecting John Keating from *Dead Poets Society* and they get Mrs Trunchbull from *Matilda* instead.

Adam Lewis, English Teacher

CASE STUDY: BEING RESILIENT IN THE FACE OF REJECTION

In less than forty-eight hours, I have seen trainees transformed from pictures of misery, panic and self-doubt into confident, animated and enthusiastic budding new teachers, simply because they have secured their first post. No one wants to fail; no one wants to be the last trainee in any cohort to gain employment; and no one wants to have endless interviews!

Finding the right first teaching post is a matter of holding one's nerve, of believing in oneself and of taking charge of the application process, which is easier said than done in the face of sometimes repeated rejection and, at times contradictory, feedback.

Some of the reasons why trainees I have worked with have navigated the minefield of job-hunting successfully are, I believe, as follows:

- Only start applying when *you* are truly ready to do so. Feeling that you should be job-hunting and acutely conscious of peers successfully gaining employment will only panic you into making unwise applications.
- Choose the school(s) you wish to apply to yourself, rather than allowing family, friends and colleagues, albeit well-meaning ones, to influence you too heavily.
- If you are unsuccessful at your first or second interview, reflect calmly on your own performance and combine this with whatever feedback you can glean. Don't just fixate upon your weaknesses; build consciously on your strengths.
- Seek advice from colleagues, particularly their views on the lesson you have been tasked to deliver, altering aspects of it accordingly, without losing the essence of yourself and your own ideas.

Repeated rejections and contradictory feedback are definitely difficult and sometimes bruising experiences; however, trainees who succeed understand that each interview is a learning opportunity. With determination, positivity and practice, you will ultimately secure the teaching post that is right for you, no matter if it takes two, three or even nine attempts.

**Catherine Shawyer, English PGCSE Course
Leader at York University**

TALKING POINTS

- What are your personal priorities for the right school for you?
- Do you have a robust support network to help with your search?
- Are your applications the best they can be? Do you have a knowledgeable 'critical friend' to help you with this process? Are you in possession of all the facts?

11 Interview advice and likely questions

Unless you have a keen masochistic streak, you will number yourself among the vast majority of the population who fear and loathe job interviews.

A little advice will lessen the acute feeling of fear and anxiety that encompasses the journey to an interview. Yet, like most things in life, if it is worthwhile, it will likely be a challenge. Embrace the challenge and refuse to be hampered by fear. Prepare yourself as well as you can and learn from the experience, whether the decision goes your way or not.

The role of teacher of English is crucial to any school. Such is the importance of English that the accompanying accountability is appropriately rigorous. A healthy, successful English department can help a school thrive and succeed like no other department. Getting an interview is often a highly competitive process, and, once you are there, your mettle is rightly tested.

We all know that interviews are an imperfect, sometimes crude, tool. Some people balk at the pressure; others can thrive in the one-off scenario.

The reality is that a varied interview day does quite accurately separate the wheat from the chaff. There are general dispositions and traits that will shine through during the process quite quickly. You may wish to consider the perspective of head teachers and

English subject leaders. They will likely be asking themselves some or all of the following questions:

- Does this candidate convey a passion for teaching children *and* a passion for the subject?

- Do they convey the professionalism and organisational skills required of the day job?

- Do they exude warmth and good humour? Would they fit into my school and develop positive relationships with students *and* staff?

- Do they have the capacity to grow into a truly great teacher? Are they willing to learn and do they really believe in self-improvement?

The interview day and great expectations

Every school has its own interview idiosyncrasies and unique tasks; however, patterns of *typical* English teacher interviews emerge. If you anticipate the different challenges, you can prepare for success. The interview day may include some or all of the following:

- **A meeting with the head teacher and/or English subject leader will typically begin the day.** Becalm your nerves and restrain your shuddering limbs and listen intently. This is their pitch – remember: you need to be sold on the school. Of course, some of this information may well be useful for the formal interview later. Ask questions only if appropriate.

- **A tour of the school.** Most typically given by the pleasantest students of that particular school, this is your chance to get a feel for the school and ask questions. Find out what they really think of the English department!

- **Student panels.** A common feature of interviews is involving students. They are, of course, very perceptive in their judgements. Be open, honest and warm, and they will invariably recognise your passion and your ability to communicate successfully.

- **A written task.** Common tasks include report writing, writing a letter to a parent or giving feedback on a piece of work. This is your chance to show why you are teaching English: namely, your unerring accuracy and your persuasive skill!

- **Meet the department.** This sometimes occurs in a formal setting, but most often it is informal, at break time or lunchtime. Again, it is a great opportunity to make your own judgement about the school and weigh up whether you are a good fit for the English team.

- **Teaching a lesson.** Teach a great lesson! Be prepared for all eventualities. More on this later.

- **Group tasks.** Many schools test your capacity to work with other staff and communicate effectively. Don't be a shrinking violet, but trying to dominate as if you are in some angry rap battle is a no-no. Put your views across clearly, conveying both your conviction and your intelligence.

- **Formal interview.** See the rest of the chapter.

Be the consummate professional

The English teacher job interview starts before you nervously enter the school at 9 a.m. As soon as you send your application, you need to represent yourself as organised and professional. School leaders will rightly frown upon an application containing errors. In a competitive field, you will likely be cut because of a sloppy application.

Ensure that you represent yourself as the consummate professional and you will stand yourself in good stead. The following tips will help you negotiate the process:

- **Ask good questions.** Candidates should be sent an information pack about the school and the interview day. Interrogate this information with forensic intent. Do not be afraid to contact the school to ask appropriate questions regarding lessons to be taught, or other matters such as required documents.

- **Don't assume anything**! Question what ICT equipment is available, the size of the classroom, etc. Query what resources are available, the make-up of the interview class of students, room layouts and more. Be prepared.

- **Bring the right documents**. Proof of identity and your qualifications are usually required. Don't send out the message that you are disorganised.

- **Dress appropriately and comfortably**. Conventional interview wear for men is a suit, shirt and tie; formal wear for women. Although not enshrined in stone, any deviation from this norm may prove a distraction.

- **Plan your journey and get there early**. Leave lots of time for unanticipated delays, such as devilishly bad traffic.

- **Bring any lesson resources and copies of the lesson plan**. There is little worse than being unprepared for such a crucial element of the day. Make this a priority.

Be warm and open and control your nerves

An important truth is that everyone you meet has been through the nerve-shredding affair before too and will empathise with you. That being said, it is only human to judge.

Not only that, we instinctively make snap judgements about interview candidates. Such judgements are formed in milliseconds and will be acute responses to your body language and demeanour.

What can you do to immediately establish a good first impression? Here are some pointers:

- Smile warmly and shake hands with everyone. Ignore sweaty palms and shake!

- Breathe deeply and consistently. Regulating your breathing stabilises your voice, so that you can maintain confident command.

- Maintain eye contact with people you are speaking to – particularly in panel interviews.

- Avoid bowing your head or adopting a slumping posture. You want to exude confidence, and your body language is crucial. Use gestures, but not maniacally!

- Speak warmly to everyone. People give short shrift to those who only speak to the big cheese in the room.

- All the above is crucial for an interview lesson – students smell fear like a great white!

- In panel interviews, don't be afraid to pause and think and drink, drink, drink.

Teach a great lesson and reflect

Almost all schools will give you a generic task for a lesson that will be broadly accessible, e.g. 'structuring writing effectively' or 'analysing the language of poetry'. It goes without saying that you should plan and prepare carefully. Here are some practical approaches:

- Contact the school or English subject leader to clarify any questions, e.g. class layout, resources available, student data for differentiation and SEN information, etc.

- Have all your resources prepared, with adequate spares.

- Plan alternatives to technology. There is nothing worse than when the machine stops! Have prepared different options for when your perfectly selected video fails, etc.

- Practise your timings. Don't be over-ambitious – in new environments, things invariably take longer.

- Prepare extension tasks in case the students fly through the work.

The lesson context

There is no exact formula for success, but there are some expected principles for interview lessons:

- Differentiate at least some of the lesson, based on the information you have received before or during the lesson.
- Plan a varied and balanced lesson, with some teacher talk, some group work or paired talk and a lively and engaging task.
- Ensure regular oral feedback is elicited, so students can exhibit their understanding and progress.

The aftermath

Interview lessons can be tricky. If it didn't go as planned, don't despair!

- Reflect on what went well – have clear examples ready to discuss.
- Reflect upon what specific things you would do to improve the lesson in retrospect.
- Be honest. It is often your awareness of how it went that is more important than how it actually went!

The formal interview: 'question time'

Many people enjoy sharing those notoriously tricky questions they were asked in interviews, but there are many standard questions that you can practise, anticipate and answer successfully. There are generic questions related to teaching and learning and then some English-specific questions you will want to consider.

Interview advice and likely questions

Generic interview questions

- What inspired you to want to teach?
- What interests you in teaching at _____ School?
- What are your greatest strengths and your perceived weaknesses?
- How would a student/colleague describe you?
- Give an example of a lesson you thought was particularly successful.
- On reflection, how would you improve upon your interview lesson?
- What aspects of pedagogy are most important, and why?
- How has your previous experience prepared you for this post?
- Describe what personal qualities will make you a great teacher.
- What particular challenges do the demands of the role pose for you?
- What are your professional development needs?

English specific questions

- What one book would you introduce into our KS3 curriculum, and why?
- What one text would you love to teach, and why?
- How would you inspire students to be passionate about reading?
- What is the most challenging aspect of English to teach, and why?
- How would you engage students in a deep understanding of Shakespeare?
- Is it important to teach the literary canon? If so, why?
- How would you promote writing accuracy in your English lessons?

- How would you develop speaking and listening skills in your English lessons?

- Describe an archetypal, *great* English lesson.

- How useful are drama activities in developing understanding in English lessons?

- What book are you currently reading?

ACTIVITY

Put simply – answer each of these interview questions. Identify your areas of strength and of weakness. Try, try and try again.

The formal interview: great answers

Many trees have been felled in efforts to give the perfect guide to interview answers in every field. Of course, different interview panels will be looking for different things, but it would be safe to assume that there are some common principles to adhere to:

- Don't waffle and speak for too long. Attempt to *read* the panel and gauge whether you have answered appropriately (consider the timing of the interview as a whole and each question in relation to that).

- Conversely, don't repeatedly give too short an answer, unless you are really stumped. Consider engaging narratives that exemplify your points.

- Aim to convey a clear sense of who you are, why you are passionate about teaching children *and* why you are passionate about teaching them English. Find your *core message*: Are you confident? What makes you ideally suited to this particular school?

- As in any good teacher explanation, compelling narratives are important. Give personal stories to exemplify your skills and successes. Was there one student whom you inspired, and how?

- Show you are abreast of contemporary educational issues and debates.

- Repeat and exemplify your best qualities and skills throughout the interview. You may want to identify key words or evidence of your skills beforehand that you definitely want to use in the interview.

Asking questions

Ideally, you should have had the opportunity to ask the questions you wanted to ask during the interview day; however, you will be offered the opportunity to ask questions of the panel. Here is some advice:

- Don't feel you *must* ask a question, if your questions have been answered. Simply clarify that this is the case.

- Don't ask more than two or three questions.

- Don't ask irrelevant questions about education for the sake of it.

- Plan your questions about the school in advance. Feel free to write them down, so you can remember them and have them addressed.

The big decision

Sometimes, we have to make decisions based on simple financial imperatives. We do have to work to live. That being said, most career choices are indeed that – a *choice*. Sometimes, you will receive mixed messages about becoming a teacher. Invariably, those who leave education have had a bad experience at one particular school.

As much as the school is choosing the candidate that best fits it, you must also choose the right school for you.

Here are some general pointers about making such crucial career decisions:

- Extend your knowledge of the school beyond the intense emotional spotlight of the interview process. Arrange to visit beforehand, if possible; research deeply about the school; scour your professional networks for extra information and advice.

- Find out as much as you can about the *real life* of the school by asking questions all day. Aim to find out typicality. What is typical student behaviour? What is the typical staff continuous professional development (CPD)? etc.

- Consider the English department carefully: Does it feel like a positive team? Can you envision yourself within the team? Would they provide you with appropriate support?

- Judge the head teacher and your prospective subject leader. These two people will have a crucial impact on your career. In the short time you have had, can you sense their leadership style? Has their explanation of their school inspired you?

- Does the school place emphasis on developing teachers? Is the CPD programme going to support you to improve? Is there a balance of young and experienced teachers?

- Ultimately, can you envision yourself working with those students, with that English department and under the leadership of that head teacher? It may sound trite, but many teachers will testify that they 'got the job that was right for them'. Do you sense you fit?

- Almost always, other opportunities will arise – make decisions by using alternatives to weigh up what is the best fit for you.

CASE STUDY: 'EVERYONE SAYS IT, BUT IT IS TRUE!'

Everyone will say to you, as you search for a job: 'you'll find the school which is right for you'. It feels like pretty unhelpful advice when you're staring at a September with rent to pay, but it is also true. The school you end up in and the people you work with will be central to how you survive your NQT year. It was completely integral to my development.

I had a number of interviews in the search for my first job. A scary thought grew in my mind with each 'no' that maybe it wasn't going to work out. Each 'no' felt like a crushing and very personal rejection. In reality, it is a combination of many factors, most of which are out of your control. All you can do is listen carefully to any feedback you're given, probably cry a bit, pick yourself up and keep going. One bad lesson doesn't mean you can't teach, neither does one unsuccessful interview.

All my interviews were very different, with questions ranging from the more abstract, 'What would you be if you weren't a teacher?', to the more typical, 'What would your students say about you?'. Regardless of the question, I think the most important thing is to show who you are.

My successful interview was on a Friday at the end of an exhausting week. Perversely, this helped. I'd done my research so I knew the school but I didn't have the time to practise perfect answers – I just spoke honestly about why I was there and my beliefs. It may not have been a perfect interview, but the school knew who I was and who to expect in September – and you can't offer more than that.

Helen Day, KS5 Coordinator

CASE STUDY: LIFE IS TOO SHORT

If you work here I want you to be happy, life's too short not to be. I love working here, that's my choice and today you may need to make a choice about whether you would be happy working at St Mary's as well.

I say this every time we are appointing a new colleague to the teaching staff and I mean it. Think about finding a job, including the interview, as a two-way process. The school you apply for will scrutinise you, and in turn you must scrutinise the school. I'm looking to appoint staff who will stay with us for a number of years at least, many become 'lifers'.

Before the interview day, when I receive a letter from an applicant who has spent the time to research St Mary's Catholic College it shouts 'appoint me!' I have an applicant who presents as highly professional, willing to go the extra mile. I want to see the applicant present their best self in person.

Interview days vary but there tend to be common elements. For example, if you applied to St Mary's we would ask you to answer an AS level examination question. I want to know that you can write coherently and accurately, it's pretty important for an English teacher. Other schools will use different activities to test the same thing.

I would also meet with you 1:1 and ask questions about how you organise your wardrobe or how you drive on the motorway when there is a traffic jam. There are no right and wrong answers to these questions, I'm just interested in who you are as a person. You bring who you are to the classroom, as well as your professional knowledge.

A successful interview is all about recognising when the person and the school are a great fit. Life is too short not to have this happy working relationship.

Stephen Tierney, Executive Head Teacher

TALKING POINTS

- What crucial knowledge about the school do you want and need to exhibit? What important questions do you still need to ask?
- How can you mimic the pressured conditions of an interview setting? How can you prepare lesson plans or interview questions in the most effective way?
- How will you know that it is the *right* school for you? Should you say no? Should you say yes?

12 Your first term in post

The readiness is all.

(William Shakespeare, *Hamlet*)

Many professional development shelves in bookshops are stuffed full with guidebooks about the first 100 days of being a leader. Journalists have written a forest full of judgemental articles on the first 100 days of prime ministers and presidents.

Why are the first 100 days equally important to a new teacher? They *set the tone*.

You may be flushed with happiness at being a fully-fledged professional being, let out of the cage to fly unfettered for the first time, but every student you teach is making calculated and often highly perceptive mental notes about your every behaviour and action. These judgements are long lasting.

The first term is, therefore, crucial for you to set the tone as an English teacher – to establish your identity as a respected teacher and to quickly erase the 'new-teacher-target' you are carrying around emblazoned on your back. My advice would be to retain the positivity that led you into teaching English. Harness the excitement of your new beginning; be prepared, get organised and prioritise.

You will, no doubt, receive a huge amount of well-meaning advice. Timeworn proverbs, such as 'don't smile until Christmas', will be trotted out. There is an element of truth in this proverb, like most proverbs. If you try to befriend students and classes, without setting clear boundaries and establishing routines with relentless consistency, then you will struggle to recover your reputation. When Othello wailed 'reputation, reputation, reputation', he could easily have been describing the life of a new English teacher who failed to *set the tone*.

Conversely, if you attempt to become a less than benevolent dictator, you risk alienating your new flock. Stick to a simple truth. *Be yourself.*

Aim for balance: you can be flexible and friendly, while being rigorous and relentless about your expectations. Ultimately, if you create a safe learning environment that exudes fairness, consistency and high expectations, then students will quickly develop respect for you and likely choose to engage in their English lessons.

As Hamlet philosophised, and every scout knows, *be prepared.*

Plan ahead

As the saying goes, *'what can go wrong, will go wrong'*. The only caveat to that sobering advice is that not planning is a sure-fire route to difficulty and potential disaster.

Once you have been confirmed in your post, you need to harness all your excitement and energy and get planning. Any new job is challenging, but, in a new environment, with potentially scores of new students each day, you need to be prepared as much as is humanly possible.

Here is some advice on planning to succeed in your new post:

- **Ask questions.** You will likely be in email or phone contact, at the very least, with your new English subject leader and/ or mentor. Ask as many questions as you need. As early as possible, find as much information as you can about your time-table, courses and specifications, class lists and student information, your rooming and resource requirements and realities, etc.

- **Visit the school**. Normally, every school has at least a new teacher induction day. Don't miss this opportunity to orientate yourself and come armed with more questions and a memory pen to pilfer every resource and document library possible.

- **Make extra visits**. If possible, visit the school as many times as you can. Meeting students and observing teachers and classes are invaluable aids. It will also ease your nerves and help you plan with greater accuracy.

- **Planning lessons**. It is hard to plan when you don't *really know* your classes and the unique chemistry you will form with your English groups. Most schools do have existing schemes of learning developed with the specific needs of the school in mind. These are a great starting point for planning. Most schools allow an appropriate personalisation and adaptation of such schemes (if there are non-negotiables about teaching approaches (e.g. marking policies) in your school, make sure you know what they are before planning), and, therefore, they are an ideal foundation on which to build your early lesson plans.

- **Reading and research**. The time before you being in post is also the time to read the novels and texts you will teach. If you have read them already, it is always useful to reread them in light of how students will respond to the text, or how you may teach the knowledge and skills related to the text. Get yourself a reading list and get reading. Also, if you are scratching around for resources, search websites such as TES or *The Guardian*, alongside as many books on pedagogy as you can afford.

- **Be prepared to feel unprepared!** A seemingly universal truth is that, despite all the summer planning possible, come the beginning of September, you will still feel frighteningly unprepared. Don't fear. This is entirely natural, and something you may feel at the beginning of each school year, every year of your career.

- **Ensure you are rested and ready.** It is a fine balance to reduce your nervousness by planning with thoroughness, while still feeling fresh and ready to start come the beginning of the school year. Ensure you enjoy some restful time in the summer holiday to steel you for what is a long term ahead.

Prepare your classroom space and your classroom routines

Many new teachers are given a specific classroom in which most, if not all, of their English teaching will take place. A great number of teachers find a great deal of comfort in the familiarity of a consistent classroom space.

Organised resources, such as reading books, dictionaries and wall displays, etc., are all practical tools that aid your preparation and allow you to concentrate on the things that really matter – your pedagogy and classroom management.

The opening term is tough and tiring for any teacher. When the dark nights of October come rolling in, it is hard to sustain energy levels. With this tiredness and the attendant stresses of teaching in a new setting, it is inevitable that inconsistencies will creep into your practice. Students are like memory masters when a small, inconsistent approach is used in the classroom. By establishing robust routines, you can better strive for consistency.

Here are some advisable routines and habits for you to develop early:

- **Always follow up on poor behaviour.** This is the golden rule of teaching. Students are acutely aware of behaviour boundaries. You need to make them explicit – sharing them in your open-ing lessons and reiterating them regularly. You must decide on your non-negotiables. You need to use the school systems of behaviour management. Following up on any incident is para-mount, otherwise why should students respect future warnings, if they think you may not execute the sanction?

- **Always monitor the completion and standard of homework.** Once more, each school will have a homework policy. Stick to it. In fact, raise the bar wherever possible in terms of the challenge you set. If you set homework, ensure that you mark it. At the very least, plan to check on the homework completion in some part of your lesson plan. Students will quickly monitor your expectations and standards. Most students will do the homework of those teachers whom they expect to address the issue if it is not done.

- **Refuse to accept substandard work.** Once more, standards are key. It takes work to monitor the process early on, but, if you make students redo inferior homework or assessed work, they typically adjust their sense of self-imposed standards for completed work.

- **Establish lesson opening and closing routines.** Humans are creatures of habit, and students are no different. I have seen teachers use silent reading as a starting '*settler*', while practicalities such as register taking are completed. By using striking images related to the topic of the lesson as a teaser, or getting students to note and discuss big questions or lesson objectives, you can ensure no time is wasted and that good habits are formed. Repetition to the point of tedium is a negative; regular habits that make students feel confident and safe are positive.

- **Focus on your reward system as much as your behaviour sanctions.** Schools typically have a rewards system – use it. Go one step further – ringing home to celebrate the wider reading of a child or an exceptional effort with homework. Parents and students love it.

- **Make students a part of the habitual routines.** Whether it is book monitoring, having students transfer folders between classrooms or getting students to monitor questioning in lesson time, get students involved in each routine. Help students internalise your group habits. Develop careful routines about

211

who is questioned to ensure balance. Make visible to students how and why they best learn, and why routine habits support their learning.

ACTIVITY

Your first term is beset by your troubles with one specific group. They have a negative reputation in school, but you also know that you have made a few mistakes in your initial teaching of the group.

- What steps do you need to take to re-establish control and change the tone in the classroom?
- How can you best harness the knowledge of more experienced teachers regarding teaching the group successfully?
- How can you best utilise the advice from your department? Can you establish some non-judgemental feedback to support your teaching of the group?

Prioritise and organise

Starting at a new school is undoubtedly an exciting time. The temptation is to say 'yes' to everything and plough headfirst into the life of the school. Experiencing being part of the culture of the school is something new staff should do. It helps develop relationships with staff and students, beyond the narrow parameters of the classroom and the office. It is crucial, however, to recognise the value of saying 'no'.

It is essential to prioritise the different aspects of your role. The core purpose of English teachers is primarily to teach great lessons. Being a great form tutor and helping students experience great extracurricular activities are valuable aspects of your role, but you need to concentrate on teaching great English lessons.

As repeated in this book, for emphasis, two key aspects of teaching great English lessons are the greatest consumers of your time: planning lessons and marking. Ensure these take priority over any other, subsidiary aspects of the job.

Being a novice means that planning and marking take disproportionally longer than for an experienced teacher. Therefore, the strain created by the tasks is really great initially. When it does ease, and you develop elements of expertise, then you can invest greater time in other valuable activities, such as creative writing clubs, organising school trips, etc.

After your first few terms, you will then begin seeking the mirage-like brilliance that is achieving a work–life balance!

Here are some tips to better organise and prioritise your workload:

- **Make lists.** I have already stated the value of lists, but, in the perfect storm of the first term, with its mysterious events that appear to blindside you repeatedly, clinging to a list is essential. Report writing, calling parents, checking deadlines, producing resources, attending meetings . . . Sometimes the complexity of the job is daunting. Give yourself a comforting sense of control by making to-do lists.

- **Use a calendar.** The school year is jam-packed with important events that you need to prepare for, attend and simply know are happening. Not only that, you should synchronise a 'marking rota' with your key events. You don't want a parents' evening to clash with a crucial set of marking due the next day. Also, aim to include some personal events in your calendar too! You need a mental and physical break from the stressful demands of the job.

- **Plan to spread out your assessments.** The marking workload is one of the key stresses of any English teacher. It most definitely affects even the best-organised and disciplined of English teachers. It is not always possible, but aim to spread out such assessments, so that they do not cluster all at once.

Aim to mark little and often, chipping away at your marking to ensure your aren't faced with an Everest sized marking mountain!

- **Work out the inevitable peaks of the school year.** Every school has its own patterns for peaks of work, such as data collection, mock examinations, etc. Aim to get the big picture about the year ahead.

- Set yourself goals and develop positive habits. The complexity of the role demands that you establish your own good working habits. Give yourself cues to help you manage your work. For example, find a place to master the majority of your marking. Is it an office? A bedroom, where the technology distractions have been at least minimised? Do you reward yourself? Is it chocolate, a glass of wine or a game of football that makes you happy? Reward yourself with some of what makes you happy.

- Pace yourself. With the stresses of the job and the proximity to millions of new germs, illness is a common occurrence for new teachers. Trying to reinvent the wheel by creating whizz-bang resources for each and every lesson simply isn't sustainable. Prioritise and focus on your core practice.

Develop great relationships

Friendships with colleagues, particularly fellow new teachers, are crucial in supporting you through the inevitable trials and tribulations at a new school. Sharing your trials and tribulations with your new colleagues is one useful way of reflecting upon what went wrong. Invariably, your colleagues will reassure you and give you sage advice.

You will be assigned a mentor and have a subject leader of English to go to with issues (sometimes, these are one and the same person). This is your opportunity to get precious feedback on a regular basis. A good mentor will share practical and pragmatic advice pertaining to your specific school context.

A great mentor will not try to mould you into a version of themselves, but instead will recognise your natural strengths and weaknesses and lead and encourage you to become the best version of yourself.

Many teachers will speak to you candidly about their nightmare classes, *unique* individuals who challenge them or their daily woes. Try to find teachers who will share their strains, but also positively see answers in each difficulty. The best teacher relationships begin with a shared purpose and passion for teaching great literature and helping young people. Aim to foster those relationships. There are enough cynics in the world – seek out some idealists who will inspire hope in your pursuit of becoming a better teacher.

You may be tempted to avoid the staffroom and to work away. The same may be said of avoiding social events to keep up with your marking and planning. You will find many times, when your marking feels like wading through a sea of treacle, that you need to avoid work and to have some semblance of a work–life balance.

Deliberate practice

Much research and popular science have outlined that it can take 10,000 hours to become an expert. This might appear a rather depressing statistic to someone setting out as a novice, with few hours of experience, let alone a decade full.

Most teachers become a very good teacher in two or three years. They master the typical early challenges we all face, such as student misbehaviour and the sheer workload of a novice marker and lesson planner. We should be positive that we can work to become better, and that, with the right practice, we can master the craft of English teaching.

There are two keys to success: being reflective and undertaking effective practice. When I trained, in the distant past, I can remember the phrase 'reflective practitioner' was used regularly. I rather ignorantly dismissed the advice as useless jargon. Now I realise it really was crucial advice.

Aim to be reflective. Approach your teaching with the mindset of a conscientious student. You have a great deal to learn about pedagogy and the wisdom of controlling an entire room with a well-placed look!

Reflect. Watch as many experts as possible. Read and research as if you were still a university student (although your time is now much more pressured, try to stick with it). Try to keep a reflective approach, be it writing a blog or having weekly chats with your mentor about successes and failures. Be relentlessly honest and open to advice.

Now, what is 'deliberate practice'?

It is not simply repetition. We can, if we do not reflect properly, repeat the same mistakes on an annual basis. Such failure is spirit sapping and sees talented teachers leave the profession.

Deliberate practice is ... well, more deliberate! It is about deciding upon a narrow area of your teaching, such as questioning, or physical positioning in the room to deal with behaviour management. Each aspect may be small in the whole complex scheme of teaching multitudes of different students, but each is important. Each provides a marginal gain on the path to expertise.

Deliberate practice requires the isolation of singular aspects of practice that are then honed and drilled until they become automatic (isolating a specific class can help in simplifying your approach). It requires regular, purposeful feedback, most often facilitated by your mentor. A critical friend in your department, or any fellow teacher, can help you undertake it.

Many schools now employ teacher coaches to support this purpose. Of course, you can do this for yourself. By writing a blog or a learning journal, you can become your own best critic. You can build a composite picture of your own developing practice.

Aim to do some simple reflections, for example, small-scale action research, such as getting a student to monitor your use of open and closed question types, over the course of a few weeks. You can seek out student voice responses to your teaching and learning decisions and more.

The temptation is to get sucked into devoting no time to reflection, owing to feeling already swamped with work. This method is short sighted. By reflecting systematically, you can eliminate lots of small errors over time, thereby improving faster and ultimately saving a great deal of time and effort in the future.

Like going to the gym on a cold February morning, for most of us, this type of practice will not be something we look forward to, but we need to undertake it for our own good. The intrinsic personal rewards can be tremendous, and this can get us through the gloomier days when we are wracked by self-doubt that we will become a competent teacher, never mind become an expert!

When we do practise deliberately, we develop our confidence and we begin to hit a groove and start enjoying the job much more consistently. Sometimes, it just requires courage and perseverance to make it to this point.

Believe me – it is worth the effort. Helping impact the lives of thousands of young people can have a transformative effect on your life that few careers can match. Giving children the gift of reading and all of its attendant benefits is a privilege worth struggling for.

'Fail better'

Samuel Beckett once famously used the line, in his play *Worstward Ho*, to 'fail better'. Being a novice teacher is one of those bracing experiences in life where we are often forced to confront our failures in a very real and public way. Despite all our plans, our efforts with marking, our meticulous following of school systems – we still fail.

The problem is not failing. It is not learning from our failures. Once more, if we undertake deliberate practice and we reflect on our actions, not lazily attribute every failure to our students, we can make tweaks to our method that will ultimately transform our experience.

For many new teachers, the concept of failure is anathema. You may well have recently finished a degree where you excelled with essay writing, or you had a career that you had mastered, but you were looking for something more fulfilling. You certainly didn't put yourself at the mercy of hundreds of teenagers every week.

Some lessons will lift you to a height that you have never experienced in a professional context. Within the course of the same day, you could just as easily have a lesson in which every best-laid plan goes awfully awry.

Failure is natural. Sometimes, it appears when you least expect it. Your favourite class, full of industrious and insightful readers and writers, can bamboozle you with inexplicable misbehaviour or a complete absence of commitment. Teenagers can be enragingly fickle.

Patience and perseverance need to be your watchwords.

Embrace the breakneck ride, hang on tight and recognise failure as an integral step on the path to mastery.

Stick with it!

Being a great teacher requires utter determination. Some people give the swan-like impression of effortless ease with regard to teaching. Like most worthwhile things in life, this apparent ease is hard earned through sheer effort and graft.

Research[1] based on new teachers on the **Teach for America** programme (the antecedent for our **Teach First** programme) has identified that the personal qualities of '*grittiness*' and determination to plough on towards long-term goals, aligned with a positive outlook, are crucial predictors of future success as a teacher. It is no surprise really.

It reflects that becoming an English teacher is a challenge, but that those with a balanced temperament and with a steely determination to get better professionally, through focused effort, reach the long-term goal of becoming a great English teacher.

If you feel like you are drowning and decidedly not waving, speak to someone about it. Don't suffer in silence.

Don't be misled into thinking everyone else is teaching with ease and success and you are the only teacher struggling. This is almost never the case. Share your lows and your highs. Some people keep mementoes of the highs – letters from thankful students, a kind word from the head teacher, etc. This helps them master the blues when the lows swing low.

Keep remembering what led you to teach English and keep restocking the passionate drive reservoir.

It may have been reading night-time stories with your father. The first time you saw a mirror into your emotional self, because you understood the pain of a character in a story you read. Remember the furtive privilege of being able to read stories, poems and plays that you love. Remember that you too will pass on this pleasure to youngsters, who may love them in their turn, and so it goes on.

Harness that feeling of deep-swelling pride when you received your degree, which you would also wish for the young people in your care, regardless of their background or family history.

Recharge in the holidays. Come back fit and fighting. Stick with it. There are few other jobs this important or worthy of such a fight.

Keep perspective when all about you are losing theirs. Know that your efforts will ultimately be rewarded, that expertise can be earned, no matter how low your starting point.

Approach the job with passion, industry and humility, and you will enjoy success.

CASE STUDY: THE TURNING POINT

The bell rattled in its casing, letting out a horrendous, unfamiliar shriek. It was the first lesson of my career, and I was in bits. Despite having every minute detail of the lesson prepared, nothing could overcome the nerves, the anxiety and, frankly, the fear that I was experiencing.

A charge of teenaged hooves came bounding along the corridor, drowned out only by the sounds of their rants and raves. I stood upright, breathed deeply, and walked towards the door to welcome them. In they fell, tumbling triumphantly into the room. Suddenly, everything I had been taught during training had vanished from my mind. I stood there, frozen to the spot.

Breathe.

'Right, everyone out of the room immediately! I do not expect to see that kind of entrance into my classroom ever again!' They went outside, giggling and complimenting each other on their ability to cause such disruption. Talia, a quiet, polite student, suddenly put her finger to her lips and shouted, 'Sssh! Miss is talking'.

At first I was worried by the fact that a 14-year-old girl had more command over the class than I did, but then I realised: Talia had listened. It may have only been one student, but Talia gave me that little bit of confidence to do the job I had been waiting to start for so long. It made me realise that, although the first term would be a challenge, it wouldn't be impossible, and it would get better. Talia had faith in me, and gradually, more and more of my students began to have faith in me too. But she was the first.

She made me a better teacher that day, but every child we come into contact with throughout our careers helps to make us better people. And that is why we do it.

Tessa Matthews, English Teacher

CASE STUDY: SOME DOS AND DEFINITE DON'TS

I cannot remember my first day as an NQT; therefore, I have no doubt I was utterly perfect! By which I mean I am confident my hair was perfect until break. Teaching (much like chocolate) can become a bit of an addiction; consequently, it's necessary to accept that you can only do your best and, despite the colour coding, reading and preparation, even your best won't be perfect.

Although far from perfection, I remember enjoying my first few weeks teaching. My overwhelming feeling was one that continues to this day: concern. At first, my concern about my NQT year presented itself to me as anxiety; I was anxious to do the right thing for my students and not to fall over in the classroom (this happened once during my training!).

Happily, the concern I feel in my final term as an NQT has altered and improved into a feeling of continuous compromise. Compromise seems to be a healthy, happy medium between stress and relaxation that inhabits (perhaps inhibits) all teachers, particularly in the first year.

As with any job there is no fixed answer as to how to get it right. I used to abhor people (especially non teacher types) telling me how to do my job, yet now I realise listening is key – asking questions even more so.

In English lessons we continually ask students to listen and to question the world around them, yet we often forget to do the same. Throughout the first term I'd advise eavesdropping, engaging and questioning everyone you can, while recognising and learning from your mistakes.

In summary:

- Don't get so addicted that you can't remember your family's names.
- Don't fall over in class.
- Don't expect perfection, but retain the high expectations of yourself and your students.
- Do engage with others, do listen and do laugh as much as is reasonably allowed!

Jennifer Ludgate, English Teacher

TALKING POINTS

- How will your classroom routines synchronise with your English department and whole-school routines? How will you set the tone in the first 100 days?
- How will you react to failures? How will you best practise to improve upon such inevitable failures?
- Do you feel passionately enough about English teaching to want to persevere through difficult times?

Note

1 Duckworth, A. L., Quinn, P. D., and Seligman, M. E. P. (2009) 'Positive predictors of teacher effectiveness', *Journal of Positive Psychology*, 4(6), 540–7.

13 Emergency English questions

Some crucial questions are not answered on training courses. They are rarely answered in books like this. The 'answer' is usually the bitter, frustrating knowledge of hindsight. Luckily, I, and many other English teachers I know, have failed and struggled so that you might have these precious answers. So, let's tackle some of the trickier issues and provide some emergency answers:

What if my mentor or subject leader ignores me and fails to help?

Every new teacher has crucial colleagues who can help make or break your early experiences in the classroom. Good support is essential. Unfortunately, it is not always given.

There are statutory requirements for the support that you should receive. Invest time in checking such requirements. Details such as the hours you should be teaching, or those allocated for specific support from your mentor, are all key. Know your entitlements. A good school with a good support system will make these clear. If not, find out – it will be worth the time.

In all likelihood, if you have a weak mentor, you can turn to your subject leader, or vice versa. If you are in the awful position of both colleagues giving you lacklustre support, then you need to seek advice and support from senior leadership in your school.

You should also look at support from your teaching union. If your school provides little support, it is not likely to be the school for you, and you should take action.

Also, look more broadly to networks of fellow new teachers, department members or online communities. Support is out there, and no new teacher should suffer from a lack of support.

What if a fight breaks out in one of my lessons?

It is the scenario that sparks sweaty palms. It is your novice nightmare made frighteningly real. If a fight breaks out in your lesson, it can be a traumatising event. Our 'fight or flight' mechanisms can sometimes override our clarity of thought. For women in particular, this situation can feel physically threatening and highly dangerous. No one is likely to feel adequately prepared.

You need to size up the nature of the fight immediately. Some fights are false starts that require a quick and assertive response, such as quickly parting the two students, followed by confidently asking one student to leave the classroom. Sometimes, a strategic verbal volley will shake students from their ire.

If a fight appears to be particularly violent, and you feel unconfident in stopping it, you should ask a reliable student to find you support from a second teacher (usually there will be someone you have in mind) as a matter of urgency. While that happens, you can raise your voice, demanding that the students stop, knowing what particular warning may shock them out of their temporary madness. At least, you should be able to control and disperse the crowd.

Such fights occur in the classrooms of teachers of every level of experience and skill. Like an earthquake, that can be an immediate and shocking eruption of anger, completely out of the calm blue of the classroom. Don't be too quick to blame yourself.

Thankfully, these events are very rare.

What if I don't know the answer to a question?

Something strikes sharply and deeply into the authority of a teacher when they don't know the answer to a student's question. I can happily plead ignorance to mathematical questions or scientific phenomena all day long, but admitting I don't know an answer in my area of supposed expertise cuts to the quick my sense of teacherly pride.

Fight the urge to fib. Rather than saving face, try exemplifying your natural fallibility. Make students see that even teachers need to look for the answers sometimes.

Get students to research the answer, or do so yourself. Set the question as a piece of research homework. Get students debating or hypothesising different answers. Some of the most interesting pieces of knowledge are acquired in such a seemingly haphazard way. Teaching and learning can be like that.

Alternatively, you can save your pride by telling students that, 'of course you know the answer', but you want them to gain the independence of discovering the answer for themselves! Pick up a dictionary; ask a friend. In short – bluff them. It is a core teaching strategy, as old as teaching itself.

What if my school CPD and training are poor?

Every teacher has sat through interminable meetings or has been mercilessly battered by dull PowerPoint presentations. Sometimes, we just have to suffer them as unfortunate occurrences.

Your training as a new teacher should certainly offer you more highs than lows. You should take one or two workable tips from a training session. If not, then pursue more support. Your subject leader should be able to expand your horizons in terms of development.

Even if you are receiving great training as you enter the profession, seek out more. As mentioned earlier in the book, attend free TeachMeets, buy the books of the respected experts (search my bibliography, for a start). In short, be proactive. Find a solution. Seek out the support you require. Some teachers fail to realise that their CPD is inadequate. Don't be that teacher.

What if an angry parent arrives in reception wanting to see me?

Your school should have a protocol for such an occurrence. As a subject leader, I would tell my colleague not to go to reception. Instead, I would help them to contact someone in the pastoral team to help deal with the situation. Or I would go myself, from a position of grizzled experience.

If you are physically caught up in such a situation, politely explain that you are busy with an urgent manner, and that you will seek out someone who can help with the matter, such as the aforementioned subject leader, etc.

Parental meetings need to be pre-planned, structured and logged. Don't put yourself in a potentially tricky position. Even with a phone call, you should ideally consult with your subject leader and be fully prepared before you undertake any planned interaction with parents.

Luckily, most parents are brilliantly supportive and would never consider such an action.

What if I hate my school in my first year of teaching?

English teaching may not be for you. You may find this out in your first year. Conversely, you may simply be in a school that isn't suitable for you. The problem is, it is hard to know the difference.

This is where having a support network is crucial. Fellow teachers with experience can typically identify a rogue school quite quickly.

A few probing questions can help them identify patterns in your experience that signal short-term issues or potential long-term dissatisfaction.

In some cases, moving schools is a must. Typically, new teachers will be expected to spend more than one year in their first school, but there is no hard and fast rule.

Once more, perseverance is essential.

What if I get an 'unsatisfactory' lesson judgement when I thought it was good?

Judgemental lesson observations are commonplace in schools. They often take on the mantle of an Ofsted-style approach. Many observations are well meaning, well informed and informative. Some subjective opinions are flawed.

Rarely should an observation be grossly misjudged, and so you need to listen with humility to the feedback. In your feedback, ask questions for clarification. Listen for any details about your lesson you may have missed. If you are still unsatisfied with the feedback, then speak to a colleague, such as your mentor or subject leader. If the judgement is grossly out of line with your expectation, you may need to speak to your union representative.

If your lesson was weak, you should be given every opportunity to redeem yourself. Even if you dispute elements of a judgement, come back fighting with subsequent observations.

What happens when the ICT equipment fails?

If you are familiar with Murphy's Law, 'what can go wrong will go wrong', then perhaps you are ready to use IT in the classroom! Be prepared for the machines to stop. Ensure that any lesson that rests on the use of technology has a viable back-up plan.

To pre-empt problems, ask to observe teachers using ICT suites in schools. Practise using the equipment beforehand and speak to colleagues about commonly known demons in the school technology systems.

Give yourself enough time to arrive, unlock doors, log in to computers, etc.

If you are in a standard classroom, then ensure that you don't always rely upon the likes of electronic presentations to deliver your explanations or set up tasks. In fact, aim to practise a whole range of teaching strategies without using any technology. For some, the technology is little more than a crutch that can be confidently dispensed with.

What will your subject leader expect of you?

The role of subject leader is crucial to a department. They set the tone for new staff and they can be a source of motivation, support and even inspiration.

Be assured that each subject leader was a new teacher once. They have faced the tricky classes, undergone the early struggles and made equally silly mistakes. They don't expect perfection, but they do expect commitment, organisation and effort.

As a subject leader, I expect to support with behaviour, moderation and general teaching advice. I actually enjoy it; it is rewarding. Very few leaders aren't open to helping their new staff. With that in mind, use the expertise of your subject leader and ask them for help. Sometimes, your instinct will be to hide your problems, but classrooms have all sorts of unseen leaks.

Don't worry that they appear tired and absurdly busy: that is a prerequisite of being an English subject leader. Paradoxically, asking for help will save your subject leader time. Getting details right, such as essay word counts, exam timings, etc., saves bigger issues down the line. Remember – the best new teachers ask the most questions. Ask away.

Remember, there will be emergencies, but even they are part of the diverse pleasures of the job. If the job were easy, it wouldn't feel so worthwhile.

Enjoy being an English teacher.

In the writing of this book, I have had the privilege of remembering the many great experiences, many as a subject leader of English, and the many colleagues and students that have formed my decade as an English teacher. Each year has deepened my determination to be an advocate for this special job.

So I end this book advocating teaching English.

Pass it on.

The passion for reading; the intriguing debates; the love of Shakespeare and poems that catch your heart; the daily successes; the unremembered acts of kindness that Wordsworth described.

Pass it on.

Bibliography and useful blogs

Barton, G. (2013) *Don't Call it Literacy!* Abingdon, UK: Routledge.

Beadle, P. (2010) *How to Teach*, Camarthen, UK: Crown House.

Beere, J. (2010) *The Perfect Ofsted Lesson*, Camarthen, UK: Independent Thinking.

Bennett, T. (2011) *Not Quite a Teacher*, London: Continuum International.

Berger, R. (2003) *An Ethic of Excellence*, Portsmouth, UK: Heinemann.

Bruning, R. H., Schraw, G. J., Norby, M. M., and Ronning, R. R. (1999) *Cognitive Psychology and Instruction*, 4th edn, Columbus, OH: Pearson.

Davison, J., Daly, C., and Moss, J. (2010) *Debates in English Teaching*, Abingdon, UK: Routledge.

Didau, D. (2012) *The Perfect Ofsted English Lesson*, Camarthen, UK: Independent Thinking.

Duhigg, C. (2012) *The Power of Habit*, New York: Random House.

Dweck, C. (2006) *Mindset: The New Psychology of Success*, New York: Ballantine Books.

Elder, Z. (2012) *Full On Learning: Involve Me and I'll Understand*, Camarthen, UK: Crown House.

Gadsby, C. (2012) *Perfect Assessment for Learning*, Camarthen, UK: Independent Thinking.

Gibbons, P. (2002) *Scaffolding Language, Scaffolding Learning*, Portsmouth, UK: Heinemann.

Hattie, J. (2012) *Visible Learning for Teachers*, Abingdon, UK: Routledge.

Hirsch, E. D. (2006) *The Knowledge Deficit*, New York: Houghton Miffin.

Lemov, D. (2012) *Practice Perfect: 42 Rules for Getting Better at Getting Better*, San Francisco, CA: Jossey-Bass.

Lemov, D. (2010) *Teach Like a Champion*, San Francisco, CA: John Wiley & Sons.

Perkins, D. (2009) *Making Learning Whole*, San Francisco, CA: Jossey-Bass.

Roberts, H. (2012) *Oops! Helping Children Learn Accidentally*, Camarthen, UK: Independent Thinking.

Smith, J. (2010) *The Lazy Teacher's Handbook*, Camarthen, UK: Crown House.

Wiliam, D. (2011) *Embedded Formative Assessment*, Bloomington, IN: Solution Tree.

Willingham, D. T. (2009) *Why Don't Students Like School?*, San Francisco, CA: Jossey-Bass.

 # Useful blogs

- My personal blog, with helpful information, ideas and resources for English teachers: www.huntingenglish.com

- A brilliant blog by David Didau, packed full of useful stuff: www.learningspy.co.uk

- Another English teacher with lots of lesson ideas and debates around English teaching by Chris Curtis: http://learningfrommymistakes english.blogspot.co.uk

- Two blogs from Zoe Elder, providing lots of useful ideas for teaching: http://marginallearninggains.com and http://fullonlearning.com

- A passionate English teacher, Tessa Matthews, engages in debates around English and education: http://tabularasaeducation.wordpress.com

- The funniest edu-writer there is, Tom Bennett, provides comedy, debate and lots of behaviour tips: http://behaviourguru.blogspot.co.uk

- Lots of great teaching ideas and intriguing articles from Laura McInerney: http://lauramcinerney.com

- An English teacher, Jo Facer, writes passionately about reading and books for the English classroom: http://readingallthebooks.com

- A Scottish English teacher, Kenny Pieper, shares his wisdom and tips on teaching: http://justtryingtobebetter.net

Bibliography and useful blogs

- A home for a range of resources and useful links by Christopher Waugh: http://chris.edutronic.net
- An English teacher and leader, Joe Kirby, writes sagely on education: http://pragmaticreform.wordpress.com
- An English teacher and head teacher, John Tomsett, who shares his views on education: http://johntomsett.wordpress.com
- A head teacher, Tom Sherrington, shares a wealth of teaching ideas and interesting points for debate: http://headguruteacher.com
- The home of English teacher and head teacher, Geoff Barton, whose blog and resources are a boon for English teachers: www.geoff barton.co.uk

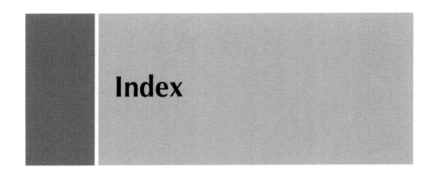

Index

Index

Index

Printed in Great Britain
by Amazon